MW01265615

LIVING WITH GOD

Devotions to Strengthen Your
Christian Walk

BILL HENEGAR
L. KEITH WHITNEY
MORRIS M. WOMACK

COLLEGE PRESS PUBLISHING COMPANY • JOPLIN, MISSOURI

Library of Congress Cataloging-in-Publication Data

Henegar, Bill, 1936–
    Living with God: devotions to strengthen your
  Christian walk / Bill Henegar, Keith Whitney, Morris
  Womack.
      p.   cm.
    ISBN 0-89900-781-3 (hardcover)
    1. Bible. N.T. Philippians—Meditations.
  2. Devotional calendars.   I. Whitney, Keith, 1946–
  II. Womack, Morris M.   III. Title.
  BS2705.4.H46 1997
  242'.2—dc21   97-11406
                                                      CIP

Introduction

What do you say to Christians whom you dearly love, who have supported you emotionally, financially and spiritually? What do you say to a church that really is not plagued with many of the problems of the less mature churches? What do you say to friends who bring you great joy, who are always in your prayers of thanksgiving?

Those are some of the questions the apostle Paul undoubtedly pondered as he sat down to write a letter to the early Christian community in the city of Philippi. This was a body of people who, Paul said, were in his heart. He had the purest kind of *fellowship* with them: "For whether I am in chains or defending and confirming the gospel, all of you share in God's grace with me," wrote Paul. "God can testify how I long for all of you with the affection of Christ Jesus" (Philippians 1:7, 8). Fellowship, after all, is not pie and coffee. It is sharing. And the deeper and more intimate the sharing, the greater the fellowship. Paul shared the grace of God with the Philippians, and he also shared his heart with them, the "affection of Christ Jesus," as he put it.

And so, in his imprisonment, the embattled apostle began his letter to the beloved Christians in Philippi. He pulled back the curtain on his prayer life and told them how he specifically prayed for them. He told them of the marvelous things, despite his chains, that God was doing to advance the gospel of Christ. And he called them to be worthy of that gospel, no matter what happened and no matter what the costs.

In one of the loftiest passages in the Bible, the apostle encouraged the Philippians to completely identify with Jesus — to adopt his love, his sense of oneness and his purpose. But above all, Paul urged them to have the same servant attitude that Jesus had and has. The "kenosis" (emptying) passage in 2:5-11 is both sublime and transcendent. The Preexistent Word, the second person of the Godhead, "made himself nothing" (emptied himself) when he became human, climbing down the ladder of humiliation from heaven to Golgotha — from the exalted throne of the Author of Life to the place of death — to die on a cross as a common criminal.

In perhaps the most triumphant "therefore" of the Bible, Paul wrote, "*Therefore* God exalted him to the highest place and gave him the name that is above every name . . . ." In a soaring climax, the apostle seems to shout, ". . . *that at the name of Jesus* every knee should bow, in heaven and on earth and under the earth, and every tongue confess that *Jesus Christ is Lord*, to the glory of God the Father!" It takes your breath away!

Paul continued to encourage the Philippians one moment and challenge them the next. He even included a paragraph that urged two Christians who were at odds with one another to be reconciled. And he instructed others to participate in the resolution process. The mission is too great, the time too short, for them to waste energy on conflict with one another.

Remarkably, though Paul languished in the malodorous stagnation of Roman confinement, there is an aroma of joy that permeates the message to the Philippians. Like a letter from a lover, his words fill the air with the perfume of peace and joy.

Just before he concluded his wonderful correspondence, Paul offered his friends some of the soundest and most practical advice they — or we — could ever hear. He said, "Finally, brothers, whatever is true, whatever is noble, whatever is right, whatever is pure, whatever is lovely, whatever is admirable — if anything is excellent or praiseworthy — think about such things" (4:8).

This is not simply theological rambling. It is not platitudes. Paul seemed to know what many of us have forgotten or never learned: What we allow into our minds makes a difference. It is very evident to anyone who uses a computer that what you put into a computer is basically what you get out. In other words, we cannot input faulty data into a computer and expect to get correct data out of it. Neither can we fill our minds with corrupt, ugly, false and sinful things — whether from a book, magazine, movie, television or other source — and expect to have beautiful Christian thoughts rising to the surface of our consciousness. The lesson is so self-evident that it hardly needs to be expressed. But then why do we fool ourselves so often? We operate as if we believe that we can feed our minds a secular and even sinful diet — and not be affected by it. Do we really suppose we can ingest anything we want and have it pass through us without any effect?

The times in which we live demand the highest response from us. We cannot afford to clutter our hearts with things that contaminate us, that are unworthy of Christ. We must see the battle lines that are drawn. As in the first century, the Church is once again engaged in a war for the souls of people, and it is outnumbered by its foes. Satan has advanced an impressive array of ideas, images and desirable things to distract us and lead us away from our Lord. We must not be fooled; too much is at stake.

In his gracious conclusion, Paul introduced a discipline that was able to transform the thinking of the Philippians and strengthen them for the challenges they faced in the first century. It will do the same for us twenty centuries later. Because it is a systematic, concrete, mind-altering *practice*. After listing those eight concepts that are to be the focus of our minds, Paul said, "Whatever you have learned or received or heard from me, or seen in me — put it into practice. And the God of peace will be with you" (4:9).

Did you catch that? The God of peace *will be with you* when you *put into practice* the things Paul has taught you — including those eight concepts he lists in the preceding verse. He seems to be saying that reordering our thinking and improving our practices can actually *bring God near.* How that happens exactly, we do not know. But somehow, as we struggle to store away good things in our mind and allow those good things to produce loveliness in our life, God moves alongside us. He helps us learn and live.

The eight concepts listed by Paul in Philippians 4:8 have the potential to reorder our thinking. Returning to the earlier analogy of technology, a person can do marvelous things with a computer if a logic program is installed. In other words, the *hardware* (the tangible device) is capable of accomplishing impressive tasks if the *software* (the internal, programmed logic or intelligence) has been put into the memory. In a sense, Philippians 4:8 is a "holiness program" for the human mind. When we fill our mind with input concerning truth, nobility, rightness, purity, loveliness and things that are admirable, excellent and praiseworthy, we are in a better position to receive God's message and to do his will. We are programmed for godliness because, when you think about it, those eight concepts are nothing less than reflections of the Holy God.

In this book, we have included a devotional message for each week of the year. And those 52 messages have been divided into eight sections, one for each of Paul's concepts. So, for example, in the first section, all seven messages lead you to consider various aspects of "Things That Are True." Following each message are seven "Reflections." We urge you to meditate on one of these Reflections every day of the week. It will help you to practice thinking about "things that are true," for example. In the course of a year, you will have read 52 messages, but perhaps even more importantly, you will have considered 365 short Scriptures, proverbs or devotional thoughts. This discipline will help as God reorders your thinking.

As you begin to read and meditate, our wish for you is the same as that of Paul as he closed his letter to his beloved Philippian brothers and sisters. "To our God and Father be glory for ever and ever. Amen. . . . The grace of the Lord Jesus Christ be with your spirit."

October 1996, Malibu, California
Bill Henegar
Keith Whitney
Morris M. Womack

Things That Are
TRUE

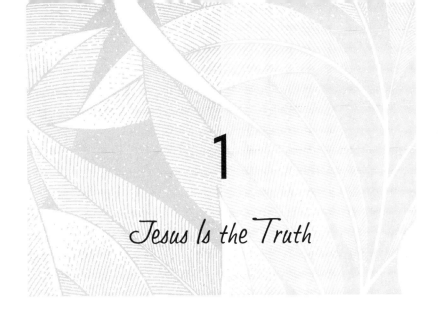

1

Jesus Is the Truth

$\mathcal{O}$ne of the claims our Lord made while on this earth was delivered in the declaration: "I am the truth." (See John 14:6 in the New English Bible.) Our concern as the followers of Jesus is to understand what the Lord means by such a claim. The saying is seemingly simple; the meaning is more elusive.

In our quest to understand the meaning of God's Word, we should always begin by asking what the words meant to the original listeners. I say "listeners" intentionally, for the Word was written to be read aloud to the assembled church, as well as to be read by individual recipients of the letters. Since those who heard Jesus most frequently were Jews, the phrase has a Hebrew background. So, we begin by asking how the Jew would have understood the words of Jesus.

The Psalmist wrote, "Into your hands I commit my spirit; redeem me, O Lord, the God of *truth*" (Psalm 31:5). He also refers to God as rich in mercy and truth in Psalm 86:15. In both these cases, and in many others, the word for truth is *emeth*, a word in Hebrew meaning fidelity, reliability and faithfulness. In other words, *emeth* conveys truth in the sense of the marriage vow, "I will be true to you."

If we understand truth in this sense, then the expression "I am the truth" means that *Jesus is fidelity incarnate,* that we can completely and unhesitatingly and without any reservations trust him. *He is the one person in all existence in whom we can trust and never be disappointed or failed.*

The text of the New Testament also has a Greek background, for it was written in the universal language of the day — Greek. In Greek the noun *aletheia* means truth as distinguished from falsehood, but it also can mean *real and genuine* as opposed to the unreal and counterfeit. Thus, in Jesus we go beyond the imitations, the mere images or shadows, and arrive at ultimate reality. He is the truth; he alone can reveal God to us and bring us to the place of reality. To say that Jesus is the truth is to say that Jesus is the very incarnation of fidelity and also the revelation of ultimate reality. Because he alone is true, he is the only one who can set a pattern for our lives. He alone is a faithful leader to follow.

In a world like ours, an incredibly image-conscious place covered with a thin veneer of shallow superficiality, impostors abound. First one guru and then another rise up to claim they have the truth. Some, like the angry, menacing militia movements, preach freedom but clothe their freedom in hatred and vengeance. New Age philosophers tailor religion to meet earthy desires and allow the freedom to live life over and over again. It is remarkable repackaging of old falsehoods by Satan. Imitations always clothe selfishness with a veneer of some kind. But, just as in times past, those who listen to the lie still thirst for more — for some true meaning and purpose, for something to make sense out of all the nonsense.

Our daily challenge to you this week is to let Jesus strip life of the shallow veneer of vanity. Our call is for all of us to give up the pretense. Are you tired of trying to project the right image? Are you exhausted by the hurried lifestyle, the pressure of bills incurred to support the success fantasy and the stress of living the lie?

You know the lie, don't you? It's the pretense that we've got it all together when deep inside we're exhausted, angry, afraid and lost. It is the false smile, the "Just fine, thank you," when our soul longs for something more.

In Jesus alone, Fidelity Incarnate, God's Own Truth, we see life as it should be. Looking to him, and him alone, we find the servant's heart and understand that only in loving others are we truly alive.

— *L. Keith Whitney*

Reflections

1. Jesus said, "I am the truth." (See John 14:6 NEB.)

2. Jesus is fidelity incarnate — we can completely and unhesitatingly and without any reservations trust him. He alone is a faithful leader to follow.

3. "The great enemy of the truth is very often not the lie — deliberate, contrived, and dishonest; but the myth — persistent, persuasive, and unrealistic."
— John F. Kennedy

4. To say that Jesus is the truth is to say that he is the revelation of ultimate reality. Andre Agassi was wrong. Image is not everything.

5. The language of truth is simple.   — A proverb

6. "But whoever lives by the truth comes into the light, so that it may be seen plainly that what he has done has been done through God."   — John 3:21 NIV

7. From the cowardice that dare not face new truths,
From the laziness that is contented with half truths,
From the arrogance that thinks it knows all truth,
Good Lord, deliver me.   — a Kenyan prayer

y

2

The Triumph of Truth

*I*t was "A long time ago in a [place] far, far away" — to paraphrase the opening line of the movie *Star Wars*. And it, too, involved a terrible conflict with far-reaching consequences. It was something like the battle between The Force and the Dark Side. However, while *Star Wars* was pure fiction, this was all too real. So real that its repercussions can be seen on the 11 o'clock news, can be seen all around us — in the ugliness, the hate, the violence, the evil.

Let your imagination drift back over thousands of years to that primordial place. Can you see it in your mind? The weather was always balmy, warm with a cool breeze, perfect. The air was fresh, unused, filled with the perfume of flowers. Sparkling clear water, sweet as nectar, sprang from some unknown source and formed beautiful rivers that laughed and splashed their ways to other destinations. Fruit tantalizingly hung from bushes and trees; vegetables grew everywhere. Sleek, friendly animals nuzzled the two humans as they explored the wonders of their garden world.

Into this "place far, far away" walked a reptile with cold and knowing eyes. When it slithered away a short time later, it had been stripped of its legs, forced to wriggle on its belly. But the serpent had accomplished its mission. It — or the evil it personified — had committed genocide. Not the execution of just A people, but the destruction of ALL people of ALL time. How did the Evil One do that? With a sword? With dynamite? With an arsenal of nuclear devices? No. He did it with words. With a lie.

The man and woman were as sleek and naked as the animals around them. They ran and danced and strolled through their paradise. The peace and harmony of the garden were like a glorious symphony of life. But into that symphony came a small discordant tone. "Did God really say, 'You must not eat from any tree in the garden'?" The discordant tone grew louder. "You will not surely die." The tone was louder still. "For God knows that when you eat of it your eyes will be opened, and you will be like God, knowing good and evil." Now the humans could hear only the evil tone. The symphony was gone.

The beautiful woman swallowed the ugly lie. She snatched away the only thing that God had reserved for himself. She ate the forbidden fruit and gave to her husband, and he ate also. And they died. In an instant, they died spiritually. And from that moment they began to die physically as they were cut off from the life-sustaining tree in the center of the garden.

But death came unseen and unfelt. They couldn't see their spiritual death. They couldn't realize that their bodies were aging, deteriorating. Not only they, but all their progeny, were now headed toward a dead end. The result of the lie was death.

Fast-forward to another time, nearer to our own: Another man now walks the earth, just like the first man — and yet infinitely different. He speaks to other men and says, "I tell you the truth . . . ." Over and over and over again, he says, "I tell you the truth . . . I tell you the truth . . . ." And to a lost and dying and lying age, he DOES tell the truth. In a world of lies, he dares to tell the truth.

Then one day he says to the people (and to us), "I am the way and the truth and the life." What "way"? The way back to where we began, to the paradise we lost so long ago. He is the way because he is the Truth. Only Truth can dispel the serpent's lie. This new man not only tells the truth, he IS the Truth! And since he is the Truth, he brings to us what was lost in the lie — LIFE!

Our father Adam believed a lie and died. A "second Adam" came and reestablished the Truth. When we believe it, we live — really live — because he is the way to life. And so, what have you and I to do with lies today? We are not "people of the lie," in the words of Scott Peck. We are people of the truth. Because truth has set us free.

As followers of the True One, we embrace the truth in every aspect of our lives. We cling to it as a drowning person clings to a scrap of driftwood. We tell the truth, we live by the truth, we dare not deceive ourselves or others. Because the Truth has come to us in the form of a man — like the first man. But this man is the Son of the Living God!

The world was broken by a lie. Jesus came and healed it — healed us — by the Truth. Truth is the real "Force." The "Dark Side's" days are numbered.

— *Bill Henegar*

Reflections

1. Consider the implications of the words of Jesus: "I am the way and the truth and the life."   — John 14:6

2. "We tell the truth, we live by the truth, we dare not deceive ourselves or others."

3. "Truth is tough. It will not break, like a bubble, at a touch; nay, you may kick it about all day like a football, and it will be round and full at evening."
— Oliver Wendell Holmes, Sr.

4. "It takes two to speak the truth — one to speak and another to hear."   — Henry David Thoreau

5. "Nothing astonishes men so much as common sense and plain dealing."   — Ralph Waldo Emerson

6. "I do not write to you because you do not know the truth, but because you do know it and because no lie comes from the truth."   — 1 John 2:21

7. "The Truth has come to us in the form of a man — like the first man. But this man is the Son of the Living God!"

8. "I believe that in the end the truth will conquer."
                                        — John Wycliffe

9. "Time's glory is to calm contending kings,
   To unmask falsehood, and bring truth to light."
                                        — William Shakespeare

3

The Empty Tomb

The guards reported that the tomb was empty (Matthew 28:11). They must have been extremely bewildered and very fearful. When the body of Jesus was buried, the chief priests and Pharisees had asked Pilate to seal the tomb. For, they said, "his disciples may come and steal the body and tell the people he has been raised from the dead" (Matthew 27:64). So, the tomb was sealed.

After the resurrection, the guards told the chief priests "everything that happened" (Matthew 28:11). On hearing this, the chief priests met with the elders and "devised a plan" (Matthew 28:12). Isn't it amazing that when the body was interred, the chief priests predicted that the disciples might "steal the body," and after the resurrection they *devised* the same story? It appears all too coincidental, doesn't it?

But, the tomb was sealed! Sealed with an official Roman seal! A guard was to "make the tomb as secure as you know how." Doesn't it strike you as extraordinary that these experienced guards could not prevent such a *predicted* event as this? The tomb was sealed! The guards were posted! And, yet, the disciples stole the body that the high priests had ordered the guards to protect.

If the disciples had stolen the body of Jesus, then at least five crimes punishable by death were committed: (1) stealing a body; (2) allowing a body to be stolen; (3) breaking an official Roman seal; (4) allowing an official Roman seal to be broken; and, (5) sleeping while on the job. Yet, none of these crimes was punished. It is not likely, in the light of all the evidence, that the disciples broke the seal, bypassed the wary eyes of the guards, entered the tomb and carried the body away.

No, the tomb was empty! No one has and no one can successfully explain the empty tomb apart from the resurrection of Jesus. Scholars are divided as to where the actual tomb of Jesus was. There are at least two sites: at the Church of the Holy Sepulcher and the place known as "Gordon's Tomb." Inside one of these tombs as one is exiting from it is a small sign which reads, **"He is not here. He is arisen."** How profound one feels as these words are first seen! Truly, he is not there; he has arisen. (See Matthew 28:5-7).

The fact of the empty tomb has great significance for us. It is the declaration that our Savior was not left to decay in the tomb; he arose in order to certify and guarantee that one day we will likewise rise from the dead. In the words of the apostle Paul: "If there is no resurrection of the dead, then not even Christ has been raised. And if Christ has not been raised, our preaching is useless and so is your faith. More than that, we are then found to be false witnesses about God, for we have testified about God that he raised Christ from the dead. But he did not raise him if in fact the dead are not raised. For if the dead are not raised, then Christ has not been raised either. And if Christ has not been raised, your faith is futile; you are still in your sins" (1 Corinthians 15:13-17).

What a tragedy if there was no empty tomb! We would still be sinners; our message about the Christ is all a lie! There is nothing beyond this world! We literally become fools for a God who truly has not provided for us what he has promised he will provide.

Christianity alone, of all the major world religions, is based on a living founder, a living leader, and a living savior. Buddha is dead; Mohammed is dead; Moses is dead;

and so are all of the founders of all of the major world religions. Christ alone is living! In fact, his church was not established until he had died, risen from the dead and ascended into Heaven to be at the right hand of God.

From the very earliest times of Christian history, followers of Jesus have celebrated his death and resurrection. In the New Testament, we learn of early Christians celebrating the resurrection of Jesus on the first day of the week, the day on which Jesus was resurrected, by participating in the Lord's Supper, or the Communion. So, each Sunday when we participate in the Communion, we celebrate the Empty Tomb, or the resurrection. Today, throughout the "Christian" world, believers in Christ's resurrection celebrate a special day they call "Easter" to honor and testify to the truth of the Empty Tomb. Through faith we join in a celebration of the Living Jesus, our Savior and our Christ!

— *Morris M. Womack*

Reflections

1. "He is not here; he is arisen!"

2. "If Christ has not been raised, our preaching is useless and so is your faith."   — 1 Corinthians 15:14

3. "If there is no resurrection from the dead, what other options do we have?"

4. "How is your life different from that of others because you know resurrection lies ahead?"
                                        — Lawrence O. Richards

5. Centuries before Jesus was raised from the dead, Job said, "I know that my Redeemer lives, and that in the end he will stand upon the earth" (Job 19:25).

6. "Because He lives I can face tomorrow,
      Because He lives all fear is gone;
      Because I know He holds the future,
      And life is worth the living just because He lives."
                                    — William and Gloria Gaither

7. "I serve a risen Savior, He's in the world today;
      I know that He is living, whatever men may say;
      . . . You ask me how I know He lives?
      He lives within my heart."   — A. H. Askley

4

Freedom through Truth

$\mathcal{D}$o you ever remember having told someone a lie? Perhaps each of us has been guilty of telling a lie to someone. Did you suffer a guilty conscience? Did you feel in bondage to your lack of honesty? In addition to telling a lie, we have all made other mistakes in our lives that we knew were wrong and which we did not want anyone else to know about.

Although it seems foolish now, I recall an event that happened when I was about 12 or 13 years old. Some of the "big boys" were going "possum hunting," and I was allowed to go with them. While we were walking in the woods, one of the "big boys" had a loaded pistol, which he offered to let me carry. This was real grown-up stuff. Sure I wanted to carry it. When I handed it back to him, he warned that I should tell **no one** about having carried the gun, for it was illegal and I might get arrested. I believed him. I moped around for days. My mother noted that I was particularly worried and wanted to know why, but I refused to tell her. After she convinced me that I could trust her, I told her. She assured me that no one was going to arrest me and that the "big boy" was just trying to scare me. What a relief I felt! That day, the truth that I was not going to be arrested set me free from fear.

When Jesus made the great statement "You shall know the truth and the truth shall set you free" (John 8:32), he had a much greater principle in mind than the little story above involves. Yet, in many ways, that is exactly what he meant. The apostle Paul articulated the blessing and power of freedom when he wrote: "It is for freedom that Christ has set us free. Stand firm, then, and do not let yourselves be burdened again by a yoke of slavery" (Galatians 5:1). These two verses of Scripture offer the Christian one of the most valuable blessings we could hope for. We *can* be free!

Freedom is a priceless possession. We often hear the expression "free as a bird." Yes, the bird does have a sort of freedom that we might desire. The bird appears to have a special kind of existence — able to soar to the heights and live above the mundane things we experience. But the bird only has the freedom to be a bird. That's all! But, we have the freedom in Christ to be or become so much more than we have ever been able to conceive. I recently heard minister Jack Hayford comment that God knew us even before we were conceived and he sees the potential in each of us much greater than any of us could imagine. We, therefore, have the freedom to become, to develop, to grow. We have the truth, and the truth will make us free.

"You shall know **the truth** . . . ." What is the truth? This is not such a strange question. Pilate asked Jesus this same question when Jesus was being tried for his life. Mankind has been asking this question since the dawn of existence. The philosophers asked this question. When Jesus said that we shall know "the truth," was he assuming that there is really a truth to be known? I think so. Our generation often flounders in a sea of confusion as many often say "There is no eternal truth." Truth changes as we learn more. Truth is what each of us wants it to be. Truth is relative to the time and place. Is this what Jesus meant?

No, Jesus did not mean that all truth changes, is what one may want it to be, or is relative. It is a fact that there are some truths that are relative; it does change as we learn more. But, Jesus was declaring that there is an eternal truth. An ultimate truth! A truth that transcends time and space! It is **this** truth that Jesus was saying would make us free. And when Jesus makes us free, says Paul, we will be free indeed.

Living "in Christ" provides us with an exhilarating freedom. We are free to serve a God who can provide us with opportunity to become. No one could have made me, as a child, believe I would experience what I have already experienced — and yet, God is not through with me yet. My mind is free to think, to learn, to grow. I can experience a freedom from fear, for if I am in a covenant relationship with Christ, I have no reason to fear. So, in a way that I can never fully understand, the **truth has made me free, and it can make you free!**

— *Morris M. Womack*

Reflections

1. "Now the Lord is the Spirit, and where the Spirit of the Lord is, there is freedom." — 2 Corinthians 3:15

2. "We are free to serve a God who can provide us with the power to become."   — Author Unknown

3. "Live as free men, but do not use your freedom as a cover-up for evil; live as servants of God."
                                                   — 1 Peter 2:16

4. "The attainment of truth is the function of every part of the intellect."   — Aristotle

5. "I run in the path of your commands, for you have set my heart free."   — Psalm 119:18

6. "So long as man remains free, he strives for nothing so incessantly and so painfully as to find someone to worship."   — Fedor Dostoevski

7. There is truth that transcends time and space: unchangeable truth.

5

On Keeping Vows

Vows in the Bible are solemn promises that bind persons making them to behave in a specified manner. The first mention of a vow in the Bible involves the vow of Jacob, who had just left home on a long journey to the land of his mother's birth, where among her people he was to find a wife (Genesis 28:10 and following). When the sun set, Jacob stopped for the night. He found a stone, put it under his head and went to sleep. But his sleep was filled with a strange dream. He saw a stairway reaching from earth to heaven. On the stairway he saw angels ascending and descending. Above it stood the LORD who spoke to Jacob and repeated the promises he had given to Jacob's ancestor Abraham.

When Jacob awoke, he trembled with fear because he believed he was at the gate of heaven. As morning broke, he took the stone that he had placed under his head and anointed it a pillar to God. There, at heaven's gate, he made a vow to give back to God a tenth of all that God gave him.

All vows were made to God as a promise in expectation of his favor or in thanksgiving for his blessings. Vowing was voluntary; however, once the vow was made, its performance was mandatory. **So vows were to be made only after careful consideration of what would please God** (see Proverbs 20:25).

Finally, vowing was described by the Psalmist David as joyful worship (Psalm 61) and is often associated with salvation (Psalm 22:22-27 and 66:13-20). Hence, Malachi lets us know that *deception in vowing is an affront to God and brings his curse* (Malachi 1:14).

Vows seldom occur in the New Testament. The apostle Paul, likely at the end of a 30-day period of abstinence from meat and wine, had his hair cut off at Cenchrea, "for he had taken a vow" (Acts 18:18, a probable reference to the Nazarite vow described in Numbers 6). Not much else is said about vows *per se*.

However, in a very real sense, the early Christian confession "Jesus is Lord" can be understood as a vow. The Christian's righteousness or justification is by faith. As Paul describes justification by faith, he notes that "The word is near you; it is in your mouth and in your heart; that is, the word of faith we are proclaiming: That if you confess with your mouth, 'Jesus is Lord,' and believe in your heart that God raised him from the dead, you will be saved" (Romans 10:8, 9). Paul is clearly expounding on Deuteronomy 30:14, "No, the word is very near you; it is in your mouth and in your heart *so you may obey it*." Our vow is to obey the Lord Jesus.

What Jacob found at Bethel, what Paul, blinded by God, *saw* on the road to Damascus, and what we find also in Jesus, God's stairway for us into heaven itself, is God's grace. Like Jacob, our spiritual ancestor, we are schemers selfishly seeking to be more important than our brothers. We are flawed and failed, foolish beyond description. But, like Jacob, by grace God chooses us to receive his blessings and promises. We throw off the burdens and shamelessly climb on Christ's back as he carries us up the stairway into heaven itself.

Our vow, voluntarily and thankfully made in response to all he has done for us, is that "Jesus is Lord." In baptism, we die to self as lord, we are buried with Jesus, and we rise with Jesus as the central focus of our lives. In vowing, as in vows of old, we are to continually ask what would please him; in living, as with Jacob and Paul, we ever and always live in response to the grace of God by living in sincere obedience to the Lord.

— L. Keith Whitney

Reflections

1. "For you have heard my vows, O God; you have given me the heritage of those who fear your name."
— Psalm 61:5

2. "No one is as capable of gratitude as one who has emerged from the kingdom of night." — Elie Wiesel

3. All vows in the Bible were made to God as a promise in expectation of his favor or in thanksgiving for his blessings.

4. What Jacob found at Bethel, what Paul, blinded by God, *saw* on the road to Damascus, and what we find also in Jesus, God's stairway for us into heaven itself, is God's grace.

5. "No, the word is very near you; it is in your mouth and in your heart so you may obey it."
— Deuteronomy 30:14

6. "Then will I ever sing praise to your name and fulfill my vows day after day."   — Psalm 61:8

7. "O Jesus, I have promised to serve thee to the end; Be thou forever near me, my master and my friend: I shall not fear the battle if thou art by my side, nor wander from the pathway if thou wilt be my guide."   — John E. Bode

6

To Tell the Truth

*I*n his book, *The Weight of Glory and Other Addresses*, C.S. Lewis accurately describes the true plight of modern man: "We are half-hearted creatures fooling around with drink and sex and ambition when infinite joy is offered us, like an ignorant child who wants to go on making mud pies in a slum because he cannot imagine what is meant by the offer of a holiday at the sea. We are far too easily pleased."

To tell you the truth, I often feel as if I settle for mud pies. Oh, I don't crave alcoholic drink or illicit sexual encounters. But I often crave popularity or honor or approval. Truthfully, I find I love being praised or preferred. I absolutely fear being rejected or rebuked. I seem to live my life seeking to please others. Since I fear their rejection or ridicule, I am often a coward who would rather retreat in fear than try anything and perhaps fail. The result is a life filled with regret. Too often, the truth is that I just never tried.

Fear seems to conquer many of us. Recent research studies involved asking nursing home residents and retired college teachers what they regretted. As with me, most admitted that the failure to seize opportunities, the failure to try, haunted them the most.

I am convinced that each of us is created for greater things. We are royalty, adopted children of God, princes and princesses in his household. *We were created to love and to be loved.* We were created for celebration and joy; we often make mud pies. We just go through the motions of living; we just exist. The resulting numbness is worse for many than the pain of failed efforts.

To tell the truth, I believe in God. I believe he is in his Heaven and in control. When I am not engaged in the business of making mud pies, I even pause to worship and adore him. Truthfully, I believe in Jesus Christ as Son of God and Savior. I am moved to tears by just thinking about his awesome majesty and the extent of his love for me. But still, I make mud pies. Still, even though I understand his power and glory, I fear being rejected. Still, I continue my puny efforts to seek the praise or approval of others. My concern is continually for me.

Who can rescue us from our futile preoccupation with self? Who or what can help us to live in celebration or on a figurative "holiday at sea" rather than in fear and futility? God's truth is that *we are living as his children when we love others as Jesus loved us.* Love in action, humbly serving, without any conditions, without any expectations, is what gives us grace and blessed peace. When we are so possessed by the Presence of Jesus, when we have been immersed so that his love floods our very souls, then our lives will radiate his love to others. When we are finally aware of our salvation, of the eternal life we possess in him, we will be moved to see Jesus in the faces of others. We will see Jesus in the unwanted, the unloved, and the uncared-for citizens of planet Earth. Then, and only then, we are liberated to life as he alone could demonstrate.

Now, don't be misled. The unfortunate truth is that mud pies are still my specialty. I write papers no one reads. I buy clothes to impress others, only to feed the appetite of moths. I build a big house so that all the toys will fit. Like the man who tore down his barns to build even bigger receptacles for his goods, I buy an even bigger house for all my "stuff." But increasingly, I am understanding that what God created us for is to love each other. Increasingly, I am able to remember his words and actions and reorient my life. Jesus tells us that God created us to love one another as he loved. Loving God, finding the heart's true home, begins by loving and caring for others. And, in this world of work and career and endless time pressures, loving God begins by loving the ones he brings into our lives. Loving begins at home!

If I am unable to see Jesus hungering and thirsting for love and tender care, for attention, when I look into the face of the spouse God entrusted to me, then how can I see to love him in the face of the stranger? If I have no time for the children God miraculously gave, how can I ever find time to serve Jesus in the face of the homeless or drug-addicted or imprisoned?

The truth is that you and I need to see Jesus in our spouses, our children, our friends and relatives. For when we see Jesus in our children, our spouse, our brothers and sisters, our moms and dads, our fellow Christians, we will be moved to love them and serve them. If we learn to humble ourselves and serve, we might just begin to realize that we are doing the greatest work of all. We are doing God's work. We are loving others. We are bringing the life-saving water of love and acceptance to someone thirsting for love.

To tell the truth, I don't think anyone can really understand Jesus or life itself until we know what it is to love another person without any conditions, without any expectations. The world has never known such great need for love in action as it knows now. We are far too busy making mud pies to love. When we love others unconditionally, really caring for them, we become *his* love, *his* compassion. We are sharing Jesus, and we are living life on a joy-filled holiday.

— *L. Keith Whitney*

Reflections

1. Love in action, humbly serving, without any conditions, without any expectations, is what gives us grace and blessed peace.

2. "Fear is the prison of the heart."   — A proverb

3. "If a man hasn't discovered something that he will die for, he isn't fit to live."   — Martin Luther King Jr.

4. "You will never find yourself until you face the truth."   — Pearl Bailey

5. I am convinced that each of us is created for greater things. We are royalty, adopted children of God, princes and princesses in his household.

6. "Be devoted to one another in brotherly love."
                                                  — Romans 12:10

7. God's truth is that we are living as his children when we love others as Jesus loved us.

7

The Last Person to Lie To

*M*ost of us remember those childhood lies. There were times when we would do almost anything to get ourselves out of trouble. Including lying. As we grew up, we learned that lying doesn't solve or heal anything. It merely layers over infected problems and keeps them from getting well. Only the fresh air of truth sets the stage for recovery.

All lying is bad. But there is one kind of lying that is worse than all the others. The reason it is so insidious is that it obscures not just the truth about a certain act or situation, but obscures all truth. It is the problem — the folly — of lying to oneself.

The person who lies to himself or herself is in grave peril. He or she is in danger of losing all perspective, of losing touch with reality. Reality, after all, is about truth. To be real is to be "of or relating to fixed, permanent or immovable things; not artificial, fraudulent, illusory or apparent." Lies, on the other hand, are a twisting or disfiguring of what is real — until, finally, what is real *can no longer be known.*

This is the slimy pit into which we fall when we lie to ourselves. It starts simply enough: At first we just lie about things and events. Then, to assuage a guilty conscience, we move to the next step and convince ourselves that there is some truth in our lies. Then we move on to self-justification. Sometimes paranoia sets in. "Yes," we decide, "I am lying, but I have a right to lie, because I am unappreciated, discriminated against, unfortunate." In the final stage, lies are completely transformed into "truth," and all true perspective is lost.

Indeed, some believe that, at least in part, this is the beginning of mental illness. Losing our grip on reality is a very, very dangerous thing — psychosis can follow. I remember hearing a Christian counselor on the radio tell about a woman who was sent to his office in a mental ward of a Southern California hospital. The woman was ranting and raving out of her mind. He decided to read Scripture aloud in her presence, and he turned to the book of Matthew. As he read the Bible, the poor woman continued to scream and shout, frequently using obscenities. Still he read on — one hour, two hours. Then, miraculously, after several hours of combat between the spoken Word of God and the babblings of a mad person, the woman began to listen. She sat quietly as the words of TRUTH washed over her tortured soul. When she left the counselor's office, she was calm and peaceful. Reality — truth! — had broken through.

It is rarely that simple to break through a person's self-constructed shell of lies and unreality. In fact, there is another element, another force we must deal with in such a situation. And that is the "father of lies." Satan began his career on earth by creating an untrue environment. The Man and Woman knew very well what God had commanded them. But Satan cleverly inticed them with an intoxicating mix of lies that appealed to their own desires and pride. "Did God *really* say you should not eat of the tree?" (Loosen the grip on reality.) "*He knows* that in the day you eat of it, you will become as gods." (Question God's motives; toy with their ambitions; get them to lie to themselves!) Satan knew exactly what he was doing. He is the master of lies.

Is this "lying to self" an unusual thing? Not at all. In fact, it appears so harmless that it often is the beginning point of other sins that result in great heartache and destruction. Lying to self is the platform of a life of crime, for example. How else can the criminal live with himself or herself? But it is *also* the way ordinary "good" people get involved in adultery or tax fraud or cheating in business or one of a long litany of other sins. At first, the conscience is troubled, but then when the self-lying is justified in the mind, the conscience is seared. Lying becomes very easy.

All of us slip. All of us sin, despite our best efforts. In this life, we never cease to be "sinners saved by grace." In our weaker moments, you and I may let a lie slip out — to save ourselves embarrassment, to embellish a story, to get our way. When that happens, we must repent and confess it quickly. We must never justify the lie as if there were some good reason for it. Because one unrepented lie can become two, then four, then finally we are on our way to unreality.

The very last person we should lie to is ourself. Because it blinds us, and we can't see the way Home to God.

However, when we *turn away* from the "father of lies," we *turn to* the Father of Lights, the God of all truth. And to Jesus who IS the Truth.

— *Bill Henegar*

Reflections

1. "If you tell the truth, you don't have to remember anything."   — Mark Twain

2. "The person who lies to himself or herself is in grave peril. He or she is in danger of losing all perspective, of losing touch with reality."

3. "The truth is a snare: you cannot have it, without being caught. You cannot have the truth in such a way that you catch it, but only in such a way that it catches you."   — Søren Kierkegaard

4. "Therefore each of you must put off falsehood and speak truthfully to his neighbor, for we are all members of one body."   — Ephesians 4:25

5. "Everyone who does evil hates the light, and will not come into the light for fear that his deeds will be exposed. But whoever lives by the truth comes into the light, so that it may be seen plainly that what he has done has been done through God."

— John 3:20, 21

6. "So it is more useful to watch a man in times of peril, and in adversity to discern what kind of man he is; for then at last words of truth are drawn from the depths of his heart, and the mask is torn off, reality remains."   — Lucretius

7. "If you lie and then tell the truth, the truth will be considered a lie."   — Sumerian proverb

Things That Are

NOBLE

8

The Untouchables

*I*t is no longer legal to discriminate against them. A 1955 law in India supposedly abolished the caste system, thus freeing the "Untouchables" from their terrible stigma of "uncleanness." But old cultural institutions die hard, and many higher-caste Hindus still consider contact with those lowest caste people to be defiling.

The term "Untouchables" doesn't conjure up images of a defiled and defiling lower-class Hindu people for most Americans, however. Instead, we are more apt to think of Untouchables as that fearless group of government agents, led by Elliot Ness, who harassed organized crime rings — especially Al Capone and his gang — during Prohibition in the 1920s. Capone's men gave those G-men the nickname "Untouchables" because numerous attempts to bribe them failed. Their stories have been told and retold in movies and on television.

Now allow me to give you a third vision of an "Untouchable." Not a disenfranchised Hindu. Not Elliot Ness or one of his G-men. But an ordinary person who maintains his or her integrity.

What is integrity, anyway? For many of us, integrity simply means honesty. That certainly is part of the meaning of the word. But integrity is broader and bigger than honesty.

Integrity is from the same Latin root as "integer." Do

you remember what an integer is from your arithmetic days? An integer is a whole number — as opposed to a fraction. The word itself means "whole," or literally in Latin, *in* plus *teger* means "*not touched.*" It is similar to the word "intact," which also means untouched, unbroken or whole.

So integrity is more than honesty; it means wholeness or unbrokenness. It means unimpaired, incorruptible, sound, in perfect condition. When it comes to people, it especially refers to being of sound moral principles — upright, sincere. And, yes, honest.

Of all the things you own or will ever possess, nothing is as precious as your integrity. Because integrity is price-less — it cannot be bought, even with millions of dollars. It is established over a long period of time, one noble act upon another. You can't wake up one day and say, "Today I'm going to have integrity." Integrity is a "track record," a retrospective analysis of the high road on which you have traveled in your life. So if someone decides to become a person of integrity, he or she begins to live a noble life today. Then one day in the future the record shows that the person has succeeded in maintaining personal integrity.

It is interesting how often Jesus spoke of wholeness in a person. In fact, his profoundest mission was to restore things to their proper order. Our problem is that we have been diminished by sin. We have failed to meet the right-eous potential that God created in us. Even after we come to Jesus, he urges us to avoid being corrupted by the world around us. He wants us to remain untouched, undiminished.

But every day, the world chips away at our character, our integrity, our wholeness. It chips away at our moral principles. The world encourages us to be small-minded, to be artificial, to be heartless, to be greedy, to be dis-honest.

The wonderful thing is, as we earnestly desire to be a person of integrity, God repairs those chips in our character and restores us to wholeness. True integrity is achieved only through the work of God in our lives. But that work is effectual only when and if we concentrate on living an untouchable life.

In some ways, Christians are like *both* the low-caste Hindu and Elliot Ness. First of all, we understand very well our spiritual "low caste" ("Blessed are the poor in spirit") and our defilement. We are, indeed, fallen and untouchable. And yet — praise God! — he touches us! He heals our souls. He lifts us up to sit in *heavenly* realms.

Second, we continue to grow in incorruptibility through God's Spirit. Like the famous G-man Elliot Ness, we cannot be bought. More and more, Satan is unsuccessful in bribing us with his lures of possessions, popularity and power. Our lives increasingly reflect a beautiful wholeness and godliness. That is integrity.

Yes, you and I are Untouchables. We were defiled through the Evil One, but now we are washed clean by the Holy One. And now we live in wholeness, allowing God's Spirit to sanctify us daily. Until Satan can touch us no more.

— *Bill Henegar*

Reflections

1. "Few men have virtue to withstand the highest bidder." — George Washington

2. "Trust is hard earned, and easily lost." — A proverb

3. "Of all the things you own or will ever possess, nothing is as precious as your integrity."

4. "In silence man can most readily preserve his integrity." — Meister Eckhart

5. "What is needed most in architecture is the very thing that is most needed in life — Integrity."

> — Frank Lloyd Wright

6. "True integrity is achieved only through the work of God in our lives."

7. "Integrity without knowledge is weak and useless, and knowledge without integrity is dangerous and dreadful."

> — Samuel Johnson

9

Barnabas People in Word and Deed

*A*s a minister I have great respect for words. Preachers and poets use words with reverence. Words not only possess and convey meaning, they *touch lives*! Words have a sound and rhythm that help us reach the hearts and lives of others. Through words spoken in kindness and personal stories of faith and victory, God is able to move people to follow Jesus, motivate us to minister to others and mature us in the faith. ***Words are powerful!***

Unfortunately, words also have the power to destroy. How many hopes, how many dreams have been destroyed by the insensitive words of family or friends? How many of God's children have lowered their countenance, slumped their shoulders and moved through life defeated or spiritually dead because of the destructive power of words? Years after words were carelessly cast into the wind, God's man or woman remains convinced that he or she is so flawed or so failed that nothing good can come from his or her efforts. Maybe it was the angry words of a brother or sister: "You're so stupid! You can't do anything right!" Perhaps the words have been spoken by teachers who, through laziness or their own lack of talent for teaching, spoke disparagingly: "You can't write! You're hopeless." And, accepting the condemnation, someone who could have accomplished much, who could have touched countless lives, spends dreary days looking down or away. *Words can be powerfully destructive!*

What causes us to speak destructive words? What causes us to fight and quarrel? How is it that we can do so much to build up others or bless others through words spoken and then, out of the same mouth, curse or condemn? How is it that God's people, who ought to be like Barnabas, sons and daughters of encouragement, can criticize and tear down others? God's Word teaches us that where you have envy and selfish ambition, you find every evil practice. What petty or jealous evil causes us to use the power of words to destroy?

Each of us who has come to know Jesus as Lord is a vessel for God's holy presence, his Spirit. But each of us is also a person of flesh with all of the inherent weaknesses of the flesh. We live in a world with numerous inducements to sin. In the war within us, the war between spirit and flesh, pettiness often wins. It wins because we read the profane. We sit in front of a television set for hours each day, our spirits drinking in the messages of sex, greed and vileness of earth. Increasingly, through videotapes and cable systems, we pipe pornographic images into our homes, homes once places of respite from vileness. Our words and actions overflow from the monster within, a monster which has grown large feeding on the earthiness surrounding us. That which is harbored within, the monster, spews forth its venomous poison of hatred, jealousy, and self-seeking lies.

How can we change? **How can we become the sons and daughters of encouragement we really want to be?** The Word of God teaches us that if we come near to God, he will come near to us. But the issue is how we can overcome the flesh and come near to God.

There is really only one way to draw near to God. We can sum it all up in one phrase — "Focus on Jesus." As Eugene H. Peterson translates Hebrews 12:2 in *The Message*, his paraphrase of the New Testament: "Keep your eyes on Jesus, who both began and finished this race we're in. Study how he did it." *Focus the mind's eye on Jesus, God's firstborn and our elder-brother example.*

When we stop to think about the purity, the purpose and the passion displayed in the life of the Son of God, we are filled with his image. When we take the time to meditate on him, to recline at his feet and learn from him, we are moved to dwell on the purity of his motives. We see the beautiful instead of the ugly. We witness one who builds rather than one who tears down. We see the noble, the true, the authentic, the gracious — the best in life, not the worst. We witness things to praise, not things to curse.

Summing it all up, we do our best, we are what God created us to be, when we are so filled with the true, the noble, the reputable, the authentic and the gracious that we overflow with his kindness and love toward others. We are filled with the beautiful, the best, when we dwell on the things of God. As people seeking to be more like Jesus, we need to constantly remind one another of our need to focus on Jesus. Meditation on the pure and lovely, on the sacred rather than the profane, must of necessity precede any consistency in our actions and our words. *Lives focused on Jesus can be powerfully constructive in word and deed.*

We are often encouraged to set aside a few minutes each day for bodily exercise. We are encouraged to spend just fifteen to twenty minutes aerobically exercising our hearts, lungs and muscles. For those who have heeded the advice, the transformation has been amazing. Life is filled with new vitality. *Today, if we would hear His voice, we would begin to commit just a few minutes each day to meditating on Jesus and his word. If we do make such a commitment, our spiritual lives will be filled with new vitality, and we will be well on our way to becoming a Barnabas, a son or daughter of encouragement, speaking with kindness and grace.*

— L. Keith Whitney

Reflections

1. Words touch lives. Words have a sound and rhythm that helps us reach the hearts and lives of others. Words are powerful!

2. "Keep your eyes on Jesus, who both began and finished the race we're in. Study how he did it."
   — Hebrews 12:2 in *The Message*

3. We are what God created us to be when we are so filled with the true, the noble, the reputable, the authentic and the gracious that we overflow with his kindness and love toward others.

4. "Kindness is the oil that takes the friction out of life."
   — A saying

5. "No act of kindness, no matter how small, is ever wasted."   — Aesop

6. "If you want to lift yourself up, lift up someone else."
   — Booker T. Washington

7. "For this very reason, make every effort to add to your faith goodness; and to goodness, knowledge; and to knowledge, self-control; and to self-control, perseverance; and to perseverance, godliness; and to godliness, brotherly kindness; and to brotherly kindness, love."   — 2 Peter 1:5-7

10

Facing Life with Courage

Facing the new year with all of its unknown possibilities is a real part of life. Life itself, for all of us, is a long series of unknown potentials — many may be unpleasant, but many others may provide great strength and confidence. For the Christian, the exciting possibility is to find ways in which those unpleasant potentials can be turned into positive opportunities for God to work in his or her life. Paul wrote, "*I have learned* the secret of being content in any and every situation" (Philippians 4:12).

I have often asked my students, "What would you want most out of life?" Their answer is often, "to find peace of mind in my life." Obviously, this is a goal of life for all of us. We are a nation, a world, that is constantly looking for the "pot of gold at the end of the rainbow." All too often, we are tempted to search for what we want through a stroke of luck or a drawing of the lottery rather than expending diligent effort to achieve our goals. Paul "learned the secret" of contentment. He learned how to place his life in the hand of God with a deep faith that God would "come through" for him.

Our God has been described by many terms. He is the "God of all comfort" (2 Corinthians 1:3), the essence of love (1 John 1:8), and the "God of peace" (Philippians 4:9). His promise to us is that he can give us a peace "which transcends all understanding" (Philippians 4:7). Can it *really* be true that peace and contentment are within our reach? Is it really possible for us to conquer the evil spirit of selfishness, self-satisfaction and greed by submitting to a God who is able to give us peace of mind and gentleness of spirit?

God is standing guard over us with his peace, a peace that is beyond our imagination. William Barclay describes that peace in the following way: ". . . [It] passes all understanding. That does not mean that the peace of God is such a mystery that man's mind cannot understand it, although that is also true. It means that the peace of God is so precious that man's mind, with all its skill and all its knowledge, can never produce it."

What a concept! We can never comprehend the peace of God as long as we sojourn in the flesh. We must be transported into that eternal realm before we can understand it. All this just for the asking!

Our world offers us a diet filled with gossip, innuendo and evil. But God offers us an existence in his kingdom where our anxieties can be eased, our harshness of spirit can be turned into a kind of gentleness that can "be evident to all" (Philippians 4:5) — and our troubled spirits can be transformed into peacefulness. What more could we ask for?

Although Philippians 4:4-7 stands alone in its message for Christians, it is also a prelude to the greater message discussed in Philippians 4:7, 8. We can never be transformed into those who think proper thoughts until we have learned to control our thought patterns, our feelings and our prayer life. Prayer is the one blessing that Christians probably neglect the most. Note that Paul admonishes the Philippian Christians that anxiety of soul can be controlled through "prayer and petition with thanksgiving," presenting all of our requests to God (Philippians 4:6). Until our knees are callused — at least figuratively — by constant pleading to our Father, we cannot consider ourselves comforted by the peace of God which "passes understanding."

The world can never know the beauty of Christianity until it is seen in our own lives. We must become a changed people. One of the "miracles" of the gospel was the transformation of those early weather-beaten, life-worn, work-scarred apostles of Jesus into a new type of person. Peter, a rough fisherman, was brought to his knees by the Lord; John, who was a fisherman but also a "son of thunder" (undoubtedly a blustery, judgmental person), became the apostle of love; Paul, the Jewish leader who set out to destroy all who claimed Jesus, came to be one of the most influential people in all of history. This is a testimony to Christ! The "peace that passes understanding" entered into these men's hearts as it entered those of countless thousands of others and transformed them into gentle, God-fearing people who ultimately gave their lives for the cause of Christ.

Truly, we can "Face Life With Confidence" if we will let our total lives become immersed in the loving presence of Jesus. It is not an easy task. But it is a rewarding one. Let your life become one that is centered in prayer and supplication. Let your anxieties be erased by your confidence in Jesus, and you can then be prepared to "think on these things," a practice that will make God's peace abide in your life forever.

— *Morris M. Womack*

Reflections

1. What does it mean to "face life with confidence?" Does this mean that Christians will never suffer?

2. How does the promise that God can give you a "peace that transcends all understanding" affect your attitude toward life?

3. "No temptation has seized you except what is common to man. And God is faithful; he will not let you be tempted beyond what you can bear."

— 1 Corinthians 10:13

4. One of the greatest gifts that comes through our relation with Jesus is the assurance that God can meet all of our needs. How does this affect the way you live?

5. Consider the words of this song as they affect your spirituality: "Peace, perfect peace, in this dark world of sin: The blood of Jesus whispers peace within. Peace, perfect peace, by thronging duties pressed: To do the will of Jesus this is rest."

— Edward H. Bickersteth

6. "Therefore do not worry about tomorrow, for tomorrow will worry about itself. Each day has enough trouble of its own."   — Matthew 6:34

7. Discuss with someone or consider the following verse: "There is no fear in love. But perfect love drives out fear, because fear has to do with punishment" (1 John 4:18).

11

Known by the Company It Keeps

*T*he bumper sticker is supposed to be humorous, but it expresses a real attitude today: "I want it all, and I want it now!" It is an attitude of impatience, intolerance and greed.

On the other hand, one of the noblest of all human traits is patience. Patience is not an easy word to define. In some ways, it is known by the company it keeps, by the words with which it is commonly mentioned. Words like endurance, kindness, compassion, faithfulness.

Paul said that Jesus came into the world to save sinners. And the apostle added that he himself was the worst sinner of all. "But for that very reason," Paul continued, "I was shown mercy so that in me, the worst of sinners, Christ Jesus might display his *unlimited patience* as an example for those who would believe on him and receive eternal life" (1 Timothy 1:16).

Paul is saying, "If there is hope for me, there is hope for you. Jesus was patient with me; he certainly will be patient with you." The best example of patience is God himself. He is not willing that anyone perish . . . so he waits.

God is the essence of patience. As the world's existence is prolonged, many count the passing years as a sign of the unreliability of prophecies concerning God's judgment and the end of time. But it is not the unreliability

of God. It is his patience. God could have, perhaps should
have, destroyed the planet centuries ago. But he patiently waits for others to come to faith. And how grateful we
are that he waited for us! So, patience is a trait of God,
and as we strive to be patient, we are being like God.

It has been said that meekness, or gentleness, is
"strength under control." Similarly, we might think of
patience as "passion under control." Someone who
waits without emotion, with disinterest, cannot be said to
be patient. Patience involves restraint. Deferred gratification is sometimes involved, as well. Our culture often
is one of instant, rather than deferred, gratification — as
evidenced by rampant premarital sex, get-rich-quick
schemes, mounting personal debt caused by buying now-
paying later, rising divorce rates and the popularity of
anything that promises benefits with little or no effort.

If someone waits because he or she has no courage, no
desire or no choice, that is not patience. Patience is a
deliberate decision. Proverbs 19:11 says, "A man's wisdom gives him patience; it is to his glory to overlook an
offense." In this case, the passion is there — an offense
has been inflicted. But a conscious and wise decision is
made to overlook the offense. Not for lack of recourse,
but because it is the wise thing to do.

Only as we grow older, do we understand how many
times people have been patient with us. We think of the
foolish things we have said and done, and we marvel at
how our parents, spouses, friends and elders have suffered long with us, been God-like toward us. And their
behavior calls for patience on our part in return.

Sometimes God allows pain and suffering to come our
way in order to help us develop patience. And when trials beset us, we have only two choices: Either patiently
bear the pain, or allow bitterness to pervade our soul.

Patience is such a noble virtue that it is listed among
those nine golden traits called the "fruit of the Spirit" in
Galatians 5:22. "Love, joy, peace, patience, kindness, goodness, faithfulness, gentleness, self-control" — the words

sound like a heavenly song. There in the middle, patience is known by the company it keeps.

Timothy was told to preach "in season and out of season" with *patience.* James tells us that the prophets of old were examples of *patience,* as they spoke in the face of suffering. *Patience* is yoked with endurance as Paul describes a life worthy of the Lord.

Restraint — waiting — is difficult. But it is made easier by love. A parent who loves a child patiently helps the child to walk. The little one falls and struggles to its feet. The parent holds the little hands, cushions the fall. No matter how long it takes, the parent is there. Because love fuels patience.

It is possible to patiently endure extreme difficulties because of love — love for another person or, ultimately, love for God. Patience is a choice we make. Always a choice. Even when there seems no escape from a situation, there is always the choice of loving or hating.

"All things come to them who wait" is an old proverb. And there is much truth in it. Patience is, indeed, rewarded. Sometimes the reward must wait until we stand before God in his heaven. But the reward is sure.

— *Bill Henegar*

Reflections

1. "A man's wisdom gives him patience; it is to his glory to overlook an offense."   — Proverbs 19:11

2. "Only as we grow older, do we understand how many times people have been patient with us."

3. "All things come to them who wait."   — A proverb

4. "And when trials beset us, we have only two choices:
Either patiently bear the pain, or allow bitterness to
pervade our soul."

5. "At the gate of patience there is no crowding."
— Moroccan proverb

6. "Perhaps there is only one cardinal sin: impatience.
Because of impatience we were driven out of
Paradise, because of impatience we cannot return."
— W.H. Auden

7. "Even when there seems no escape from a situation,
there is always the choice of loving or hating."

12

Our Noble Commitment

*I*t takes real moral and spiritual character to be a committed person. The word translated as "noble" in Philippians 4:8 literally means "venerable, worthy of honor." When we commit ourselves to the service of Jesus Christ, it becomes a **noble** or venerable action on our part; hence, we can truly call it our "Noble Commitment."

One of the tragedies of our day is that far too few people are really willing to commit themselves. How many times do we read of individuals who refuse to help others who are hurting because "I don't want to get too involved"? In our large cities, people often watch a heinous crime against another person and yet do not become involved — not even in calling the police. Far too few of us refuse to let ourselves become involved.

I am reminded of one of the great statements of faith made by the apostle Paul. "Of this gospel I was appointed a herald and an apostle and a teacher. That is why I am suffering as I am. Yet I am not ashamed, because I know whom I have believed, and am convinced that he is able to guard what I have entrusted [or "committed"] to him for that day" (2 Timothy 1:11, 12). Paul had a deep commitment to what he believed. He gave up all that he had, counting it as "rubbish" (Philippians 1:8) "that I might gain Christ." This is an illustration of what our "noble commitment" ought to be.

How can we attain that kind of commitment? It is not given as a mere gift from God. That would dismiss our need to be involved from being committed. It is certainly not something that we can purchase. It is not something that our brothers and sisters in Christ can supply us with. Commitment is gained by our deep faith that God **really IS** and our placing our lives at his feet.

Paul had every reason to refuse to follow Christ from the human point of view. He states that he knows what it is both to have plenty and to be in want. Before his commitment to Christ, from the worldly point of view, he "had it made." He was an emissary of the high priest, was a member of the strictest sect of the Jews, was a well-educated teacher and had considerable influence and we assume, was financially well-to-do. But all of this was sacrificed at the altar of commitment. He gave all of this up to follow Christ. This is the meaning of "noble commitment."

How can you and I develop a deeper level of commitment? Certainly, there is no easy solution, but some suggestions can be made. First, **we must desire a deeper level of commitment**. Most of us who have a shallow commitment are satisfied with where we are. That is, we are willing to stay where we are because it takes too much effort to change. The *status quo* is usually easier to maintain than to begin some drastic change in our life patterns. Until you **want** to be more committed, you will not **be** more committed.

Second, **commitment means that we must have faith in something that will control our minds and actions.** Remember, Paul stated "I know whom I have believed, and am convinced that he is able to guard what I have entrusted [or "committed"] to him" (2 Timothy 1:12). Is your faith the kind that will cause you to give up what is a hindrance to spiritual growth? Or, are you waiting for God to send some kind of special working to make you committed? If it is the latter, forget it! That is not going to happen.

Third, **commitment comes from involvement.** Many years ago, I read a newspaper article in which the writer was describing how we can develop love for another. He said, "Act as though you love the person and you will come to love her/him unconsciously." In the same manner, I would suggest that you get yourself involved in whatever you need to develop commitment, and you will often become committed unconsciously. Being committed to someone or something is what may be described as "tough love." It is not easy to come by, but when you have practiced it, you will feel much better about yourself.

Paul suggests that we practice things that are noble. I suggest to you that it is a noble thing for us to be deeply committed; hence, the title, "Our Noble Commitment." Your life will be much more satisfying, your activities will be much more significant, and your purposes will have much more meaning to you if you will "practice the art of noble commitment."

— *Morris M. Womack*

Reflections

1. Science may have found a cure for most evils; but it has found no remedy for the worst of them all — the apathy of human beings.

2. Act as though you are committed, and you may find yourself developing commitment.

3. "All to Jesus I surrender, All to Him I freely give."
   — Judson W. Van DeVenter

4. "To live a life half dead, a living death."
   — John Milton

5. "If anyone would come after me, he must deny himself and take up his cross and follow me. For whoever wants to save his life will lose it, but whoever loses his life for me will find it" (Matthew 16:24, 25). What did Jesus mean by this?

6. "Thou art the Potter, I am the clay.
    Mold me and make me After thy will,
    While I am waiting, Yielded and still."
                                        — Adelaide Pollard

7. "I know whom I have believed, and am convinced that he is able to guard what I have entrusted [or committed] to him for that day."   — 2 Timothy 1:11, 12

13

Character: The Heart and Soul of It All

*D*wight L. Moody has given us an interesting definition of character. He said, "Character is what you are in the dark." As a college teacher, I would say that character is what you are when you are in college a thousand miles from home. Character is defined by what you do when no one is looking.

Being of good character means doing the right thing even when we want something else or fear what might happen to us if we do the right thing. Character properly developed keeps us from fulfilling our lustful desires and using someone for our pleasure just because we want to experience the feelings of pleasure. Character that pleases my Lord and Master is consistency in right living, which is born out of the desire to please God, commitment to righteousness and daily discipline.

I am convinced that character is something that is developed only by years of consistent practice. It isn't something you are just born with. Oh, some people are naturally more loving and considerate than others. Some are perhaps more honest. Each of us has our own unique weakness of the flesh. Some of us have little difficulty with sexual purity, but we struggle with basic honesty as we exaggerate our accomplishments in hopes of impressing others. Some of us may never lie, cheat or steal, but we struggle greatly with generosity, kindness or forgiveness.

Our ultimate goal as Christians is to allow God to form in us character that naturally and consistently does the right thing. But how? Isn't that the ultimate question? How can God change our natural inclinations? How is character formed?

Paul, the apostle, wrote to the church at Rome, "...we also rejoice in our sufferings, because we know that suffering produces perseverance; perseverance, character; and character, hope" (Romans 5:4). Character development is a lengthy, sometimes painful process. It comes through the experience of failure and frustration.

Perhaps that is what Charles Reade means when he writes: "Sow an act and reap a habit. Sow a habit and you reap a character. Sow a character and you reap a destiny." Character is generally formed in the crucible of pain and failure. Character is formed when we suffer the consequences of our sin or of someone else's.

Rather than tell you a story about my own life or violate a confidence and tell about someone else, I will use the wonderful story of *The Velveteen Rabbit*, a children's story written by Margery Williams. Again, character is what we *really* are and not what we pretend to be when someone is looking. Rabbit sets up the teachable moment with the critical question, "What is Real?"

"What is real?" asked Rabbit one day, when they were lying side by side near the nursery fender, before Nana came to tidy the room. "Does it mean having things that buzz inside you and a stick-out handle?"

"Real isn't how you are made," said the Skin Horse. "It's a thing that happens to you. When a child loves you for a long, long time, not just to play with, but *really* loves you, then you become Real."

"Does it hurt?" asked the Rabbit.

"Sometimes," said the Skin Horse, for he was always truthful. "When you are Real you don't mind being hurt."

"Does it happen all at once, like being wound up,"

he asked, "or bit by bit?"

"It doesn't happen all at once," said the Skin Horse. "You become. It takes a long time. That's why it doesn't often happen to people who break easily, or have sharp edges, or who have to be carefully kept. Generally, by the time you are Real, most of your hair has been loved off, and your eyes drop out and you get loose in the joints and very shabby. But these things don't matter at all, because once you are Real you can't be ugly, except to people who don't understand."

What kind of person do you want to be? Do you have a strong desire for excellence of character? Are you willing to make a commitment to consistently do the right thing? And, most importantly, are you willing to discipline yourself daily, to practice, practice, practice love and good deeds. Remember. *Sow a character, and you reap a destiny!*

— *L. Keith Whitney*

Reflections

1. "Character is what you are in the dark."— Dwight L. Moody

2. ". . . we also rejoice in our sufferings, because we know that suffering produces perseverance; perseverance, character; and character, hope."
   — Romans 5:4

3. Character is generally formed in the crucible of pain and failure.

4. "Sow an act and reap a habit. Sow a habit and you reap a character. Sow a character and you reap a destiny."   — Charles Reade

5. "We are what we repeatedly do."   — Aristotle

6. "The final forming of a person's character lies in their own hands."   — Anne Frank

7. "Fix your thoughts on what is true and honorable and right. Think about things that are pure and lovely and admirable. Think about things that are excellent and worthy of praise. Keep putting into practice all you learned . . . ."   — From Philippians 4:8-9 NLT

Things That Are
RIGHT

14

God Alone Is Right

Our society has developed some disturbing features. In a world that is controlled by an existential way of thinking, we seem to want a standard of right and wrong that fits in with our own selfish likes and dislikes. The "you-can't-tell-me-what-to-do" attitude seems to pervade much of American culture and perhaps much of the world's way of thinking. The existential way of thinking causes many to believe that "if it feels good, do it."

There must be an eternal system of right and wrong to guide us through our sojourn on earth. When Jesus was addressed as "Good Master," he replied, "Why do you call me good? No one is good — except God alone" (Mark 10:18). Jesus is telling us that God alone is good. If God alone is good, does this not mean that God alone is right?

It is necessary to have some kind of standard by which we can determine what is right and wrong. God is that Standard. When people become a law unto themselves, there is always the danger that they develop an anarchy. Paul clearly stated that he would not have known what was right if there had not been the Law of Moses under which he lived for much of his life. He stated: "I would not have known what sin was except through law. For I would not have known what it was to covet if the law had not said, 'Do not covet'" (Romans 7:7). Not only is Paul declaring that the law of Moses made him aware of what sin is, but he is also inferring that there is a standard of right. God is the author of that standard of right; therefore he alone is right.

Our society is suffering because of the rejection of a standard of right. When individuals become a law to themselves, then those persons can do **anything** that they want to do. It is not wrong to them because they have become the standard of right and wrong. Our schools, communities, justice systems, churches and families are greatly affected by such a system that says "I can do anything I want to. It is none of your business what I do."

Crimes committed by youth are at an all-time high, especially major crimes. Is there any way that we can identify the cause of this? I believe it is because the family has broken down and no longer gives the children any sense of right and wrong. "If someone differs with you, kill him. After all," some youth claim, "it is as much my **right** to do what I want to as it is any one else's. After all, no one is going to tell me what to do." This standard of right is doomed to destroy society as we know it.

This kind of attitude of right and wrong permeates our communities. If there is something that I want, I have the right to claim it, it is argued. We just hire an attorney and sue someone. Or, we will **take** what some one else has for our own use. The old rule, "What is yours is mine, and I will take it if I want it" is the way many people think today. Many communities no longer have the sense of "community" as many of us remember them to have had.

Churches are plagued with the same problems. "I have the right to interpret the Bible as I want it to be interpreted," say many current Christians. After all, what right does someone have to tell me what the Scriptures mean. I will understand it as I want to. We have created new hermeneutics (systems or methods of interpretation) to give us the ability to place our own meaning on Scripture. Church leadership often means nothing to our generation. It is argued that no one has the right to tell me that I am wrong. When this kind of attitude permeates the church, it is doomed to failure.

Again, we must return to our basic assumption: God alone is right. If he is the Creator of all that is (and, I certainly believe he is), then he has the right to do as he will with it. After all, didn't the Psalmist record God as saying, "I have no need of a bull from your stall or of goats from your pens, for every animal of the forest is mine, and the cattle on a thousand hills" (Psalm 50:9, 10). God does not owe us anything, but he has the right to demand **all** from us. After all, God **alone** is right.

— *Morris M. Womack*

Reflections

1. "Let no man presume to think that he can devise any plan of extensive good, unalloyed and unadulterated with evil." — Charles Calib Colton

2. How can we know that there is an eternal system of right or goodness?

3. Consider this statement: If God alone is good, then God alone is right.

4. "Like D.L. Moody, we should be ready to say, 'God said it. I believe it. That settles it.' When God has spoken, there is no more to say." — Lawrence O. Richards

5. If God is truly the Creator, he has every reason to claim to be the only "good one."

6. "For everything God created is good." — 1 Timothy 4:4

7. "What a mighty God we serve,
    What a mighty God we serve,
    Angels bow down before Him,
    Heaven and Earth adore Him;
    What a mighty God we serve."— Traditional chorus

15

Justification Makes Straight

$\mathcal{S}$everal years ago, I stood watching carpenters justify the laminated beams for a new church building. *Justify* beams? What they were doing was making them straight. When we "justify" the right margins of a manuscript, we are actually making the right margin straight. When we *justify* beams on a building, we make them straight or plumb. This is specifically what Christ did to our lives when he died on the cross. He literally made our lives straight.

The words from which "righteousness" and "justification" are translated come from the same Greek root. Hence when one is made righteous, that person is justified. That person has been "made straight." The apostle Paul states that "the result of one act of righteousness was justification that brings life for all men" (Romans 5:18).

Without Christ and his sacrifice, we would be nothing. Our sins would overwhelmingly condemn us. "He came and preached peace to you who were far away and peace to those who were near. For through him we both have access to the Father by one spirit" (Ephesians 2:17, 18). Earlier, Paul had written to the Gentiles that before Christ, "you were separate from Christ, excluded from citizenship in Israel and foreigners to the covenants of the promise, without hope and without God in the world" (Ephesians 2:12). What a predicament we would be in:

lost, undone, without God! But, Christ made us straight! Christ justified us!

Our justification does not come from anything we have done. There was nothing we could do. In the words of Meister Eckhart: "One should not always think so much about what one should do, but rather what one should be. Our works do not ennoble us; but we must ennoble our works." Works alone cannot save anyone. There is nothing that we can do to merit any of God's special gifts to us. For this reason, Paul states that "it is by grace you have been saved, through faith — and this not from yourselves, it is the gift of God — not by works so that no one can boast. For we are God's workmanship, created in Christ Jesus to do good works, which God prepared in advance for us to do" (Ephesians 2:8-10). Note that Paul states that we are saved by grace — through faith — to do good works. It is not an earned salvation, nor is it given with no responsibilities on our part. We must respond to God's grace through works of obedience.

But what does this grace do for us. Does it give license for us to sin? Paul was fearful that some would conclude that grace could be increased if we sinned more. He asked, "What shall we say then? Shall we go on sinning so that grace may increase?" Then he answers his own question with the strongest possible negative: "By no means! We died to sin; how can we live in it any longer?" (Romans 6:1,2).

We have been justified — made straight — through the blood of Jesus. Paul exclaims that "There is now no condemnation for those who are in Christ Jesus." For, he says, "Through Christ Jesus the law of the Spirit of life set me free from the law of sin and death" (Romans 8:1, 2).

Since we have been made straight (or, justified) through Jesus Christ, we have many blessings. **We no longer live in fear.** When we lived in sin, there was reason for fear; for we were spiritually naked in the presence of God. But, now we have been clothed with Christ; we have "put on Christ" or been "clothed with Christ" (see

Galatians 3:26,27). As a child of God, we no longer fear God in the sense that we are *afraid, or scared,* of him; we fear him only in that we reverence and respect his majesty.

Since we are justified, **we live in the family as sons and daughters of God.** "You are all sons of God through faith in Christ Jesus" (Galatians 3:26). The sense of belonging to God brings to us that sense of comfort and care that comes from the nurture of a family.

Since we are justified, **we are freed from the legal demands of law.** We now live in the very presence of God. The Spirit frees us from our fleshly nature. We are clothed with a spiritual nature. The Spirit of God dwells in us, comforts us and guides us as we prepare to make our eternal home with God. And Paul states that if the Spirit of God lives in us, "he who raised Christ from the dead will also give life to your mortal bodies through his Spirit, who lives in you" (Romans 8:11).

— *Morris M. Womack*

Reflections

1. What does the fact that "God made us straight by the cross" mean to you?

2. "The soul who sins is the one who will die. The son will not share the guilt of the father, nor will the father share the guilt of the son."   — Ezekiel 18:20

3. What does it mean to be "clothed with Christ"? (see Galatians 3:26, 27)

4. "You are all sons of God through faith in Christ Jesus, for all of you who were baptized into Christ have clothed yourself with Christ."   — Galatians 3:26, 27

5. Consider the statement, "There is nothing we can do to earn any of God's special gifts to us."

6. How will being more interested in form than in spirit affect your relation to God?

7. Consider the verse, "For I tell you that unless your righteousness surpasses that of the Pharisees and the teachers of the law, you will certainly not enter the kingdom of heaven" (Matthew 5:20).

16

Let Justice Roll Down

*W*hen I was a lad, "justice" had a negative connotation for me. When preachers would talk about the (ahem) "justice of God," it sounded like such an ominous thing. When I heard that we would "fall into the hands of a just God," it produced a sense of fear into my heart.

"Righteousness" was one idea; "justice" was another. In fact, many have used these two words almost as opposites. We often think of righteousness with some sort of "warm, fuzzy" feeling, while justice is the work of a "just" God who is bent on assigning punishment to those who disobey him.

Years later, more study of God's word has led me to believe that "righteousness" and "justice" are a part of the same theme. In Amos 5:24, the prophet spoke out against the shallow, pretentious lives of many of the Israelites of his time. He climaxed his rebuke for their unacceptable worship with these famous words, "But let justice roll on like a river, righteousness like a never-failing stream."

Martin Luther King, Jr., made these words famous in his rhetoric of the civil rights movement. Specifically, in his "I Have A Dream" speech, he cried out these words when he called for a change in the treatment of his people. He certainly did not see "justice" as a negative attitude or as being greatly different from righteousness.

In the New Testament, these two words are very close-ly related. "Justice," translated from *dikaios* or *dike*, usually has the connotation of outward response to God's laws and living in accordance with them, while "right-eousness," translated from *dikaiosune*, is more of an inward quality of uprightness. Even the casual reader can observe a very close resemblance between the two words. They are from the same root word, namely *dike*.

All too often in our own day, we find ourselves not identifying with this great theme of Amos. We often find ourselves trying to "look like" we are righteous while not really being committed to the real meaning of right-eousness. James Smith comments: "'Justice' goes beyond fairness. It is that correct moral practice in daily and per-sonal and social life which is clearly observable to others. 'Righteousness' is mainly internal. It is that disposition to do what is right. Righteousness expresses itself in soci-ety as justice" (*The Minor Prophets*, p. 175).

Amos charged the Israelites with being more inter-ested in form than spirit, more focused on obedience of a code of laws than on dedicating their lives in service to God. He rebuked them for their meaningless sacrifices; he rebuked them for their religious feasts and assemblies. It was not that God did not want them to offer sacrifices, or to obey his law, or even to celebrate their religious feasts which God had imposed on them, nor even their assemblies in the name of God. All of these things were good. Amos condemned them because they were mean-ingless. Their inner lives were so different from their out-ward appearance. They appeared to be captivated by the form and ritual of their religion, but their hearts did not appear to be committed to God.

How much we are like them! In the words of Jesus regarding the Pharisees: "You give a tenth of your spices — mint, dill and cummin. But you have neglected the more important matters of the law — justice, mercy and faithfulness" (Matthew 23:23). We are often so care-ful to see that we do everything "right," but we have lost the real spirit of Christianity. In fact, many of us often practice "churchanity" and call it "Christianity." When we do, our lives are no different than those of the Pharisees, or of the Israelites of Amos' day.

There is a growing tendency in our society and in the minds of many Christians today to ask, "What do I have to do to please God? Or do I really have to do 'such and such' in order to be a good citizen, or to be a good Christian?" The God-centered mind will, on the other hand, ask, "How much can I do?" When we have been so tremendously blessed by a God who loved us enough to sacrifice his Son for us, we should be looking for more ways to serve. A life motivated by love is a life that is service-minded.

Promise yourself that in the spirit of Amos 5:24 you will "let justice roll on like a river, righteousness like a never-failing stream!" Then, and only then, do we have a right to believe that we are living a love-motivated life. Then, we will stand out to the world as a "light" that cannot be hidden.

— *Morris M. Womack*

Reflections

1. Compare the "righteousness" that Amos preached with the righteousness of the Pharisees discussed in Matthew 23.

2. Consider James Smith's statement that justice is "that correct moral practice in daily and personal and social life which is clearly observable to others."

3. How can we make our "obedience" to God meaningless to God as the people of Amos' day did?

4. How can it be said that a life that is "motivated by love is a life that is service-minded"?

5. How can we "let justice roll on like a river" in our lives?

6. How can it be said that through the cross, Christ made us straight?

7. "God presented him [Christ] as a sacrifice of atonement, through faith in his blood. He did this to demonstrate his justice. . . . he did it to demonstrate his justice at the present time, so as to be just and the one who justifies the man who has faith in Jesus."
— Romans 3:25, 26

17

Practicing Fairness

*H*is name is Clyde. He was raised in rural Tennessee, and though he hasn't lived there in many decades, it is still in his blood. His honesty, practicality, diligence and compassion are straight out of mid-America. But the one word I would use to describe my friend is "fair." Somehow — perhaps from that Tennessee soil as he worked the farms and ranches — he developed a nearly instinctive sense of fairness.

Today, I find a *lack of* fairness that seems characteristic of our age. It is exhibited in rampant cheating in schools, ugly litter on the highways, runaway numbers of lawsuits, widespread greed and violence, growing pop-ulations of poor — the list could go on. Lack of fairness is apparent in the decay we see in our homes, our political, legal and educational systems . . . even in our churches.

Fairness has to do with justice. But it is more than our usual definition of justice. The justice system may declare an action legal or appropriate under law — and yet that action can remain unfair or unjust. That is because fairness goes to a deeper moral and ethical level. We don't learn fairness from law books. We learn it in places like rural Tennessee in the late 1940s.

Very early, Clyde developed a keen sense of fairness. Obviously, much of that special sense came from his train-ing at home. It also came from his years in church and

Bible school. Even the public schools in that day seemed concerned with the meaning of fairness. But after you are taught to be fair, you still must *believe* it is *right* to be fair. You must *practice* fairness in your everyday thinking and behavior — even when nobody is watching.

A sense of fairness goes to the very core of who or what we are as people. A person can do wonderful deeds, be civic-minded, be a good neighbor, yet still not have a deep abiding sense of true justice or fairness. Fairness has to do with the way things *ought* to be. It is an understanding, a judgment of what is right. Rightness is a trait of God. And so is fairness, which is nearly the same. When we struggle within our conscience to be fair or just, we are like God. We are godly people.

Clyde grew up in a part of the country that discriminated against African Americans in the 1940s. But as he left home for the Navy and encountered people of different cultures and races, that down-home prejudice didn't square in his mind with what he had been taught about fairness. His sense of what is right seemed to also call for *consistency* — not merely fairness in dealing with most people, but the *same* fairness for *all* people. As a result, he became one of the most accepting individuals I have ever known.

There is a story about fairness that I like. Seems there was a baker who bought his butter from one particular farmer. The baker began to suspect that the farmer was shorting him, so he carefully weighed the butter for a week. He was right: The amount that was supposed to be a pound, was less than a pound. Angrily, he hauled the farmer into court. The judge asked the farmer if he used standard weights for measuring his butter. The farmer answered that he did not. The judge said, "Then how do you measure your butter?" The farmer said, "Your Honor, when the baker began buying butter from me, I decided to buy his bread. So I just measure my butter by placing his one-pound loaf of bread on the other side of the balance scale."

Although there is much inequity in the world, the supreme moment of fairness is coming — it is called Judgment Day. On that day, God will make all things right. It isn't fair for some people to indulge themselves in wasteful excesses, while millions suffer in hunger. It isn't fair for the stronger to rape and kill the weaker. It isn't fair for some to cheat and win, while others obey the rules and lose. It isn't fair . . . but it will be made right. God will *right all wrongs.*

In the meantime, you and I have a choice. We can examine each situation and ask: "What is the right thing to do? What is fair?" God will develop in us a sense of fairness nearly as strong as our senses of touch, taste, smell, hearing and sight. Or we can look out for "ol' number one" and ignore true justice.

The rewards of fairness often have to wait until the next world. But even in this present world, I can tell you this: When you are looking for a friend, you want someone who will do what is right, who will be fair. Someone like my friend, Clyde. And in order to have a friend like that, you have to be that same kind of a friend in return.

Fairness is a beautiful trait in a friend. It is also beautiful in you.

— *Bill Henegar*

Reflections

1. "Blessed are those who hunger and thirst for righteousness, for they will be filled."   — Matthew 5:6

2. "On that day, God will make all things right."

3. "They are cheated most who cheat themselves."
                                        — Danish proverb

4. ". . . that in this matter no one should wrong his brother or take advantage of him."
                                    — 1 Thessalonians 4:6

5. "A sense of fairness goes to the very core of who or what we are as people."

6. "Those who clearly recognize the voice of their own conscience usually recognize also the voice of justice."
                                    — Alexander Solzhenitsyn

7. "Only the actions of the just Smell sweet and blossom in their dust."   — James Shirley

18

The Judgment of God

*H*aving practiced law, having thought about law and justice, and having taught law, I have often considered it natural to think about the judgment of God almost in a legal sense. In fact, God's judgment falls into two categories: end-time judgment and disciplining judgment. I have a tendency to think only about *end-time* judgment when the eternal destiny of persons will be determined. It is like a capital murder case. Judged innocent, you are forever free; found guilty, your life is forever lost.

However, God intends much of his judgment to correct and discipline us in this life. God's love for us is *tough love*, which works to bring us back into a faithful relationship with him. God disciplines us in the hopes that such discipline will rehabilitate us and cause us to be reclaimed as his child and heir.

Thank God that *his* philosophy of judgment is not like the tendency of modern courts. We have failed to rehabilitate most offenders who have been convicted, so modern penal philosophies have moved toward simple punishment goals. God loves us enough to discipline us. His judgment means that he takes sin seriously. Sin, disobedience to the Creator, always hurts, always causes trouble, or it leads to the destruction of our souls. It eats away at our purity until we become jaded and failed.

Lawyers are often more concerned about who the

judge is than what the law or the evidence is. Our holy
God renders judgments that are always fair, just and
right. Also, our judge, who came into this world fully
human as well as divine, understands exactly who we are
and what our struggles are. John recorded the words of
Jesus: "I have come to judge the world. I have come to
give sight to the blind and to show those who think they
see that they are blind" (John 9:39 NLT). In Jesus, the man
by whom God will judge the world in righteousness (Acts
17:31), we experience a judge who has been tempted in
everything just as we are. Even though he lived sinlessly,
he is uniquely qualified to empathize with our many
weaknesses. His judgments correct us and call us to live
righteously. Our compassionate judge, ever seeking to
reclaim us as his children, ever hoping to restore us to his
family, disciplines us to bring us to sanity. Loving
demands judgment that chastens and calls us to repen-
tance.

In fact, judgment that is corrective is crucial to a fresh
encounter with God and his righteousness. God's discipline is designed to rehabilitate. He wants the blind to see
and understand. He wants us to cry for help and to experience revival.

Some faculty and students of the School of Law at
Pepperdine University spend time working with incar-
cerated juvenile offenders. Most of those who are jailed
in the facility near our campus are already hardened.
They think they know it all. They are street-wise and cyn-
ical. They think they can con anyone, even those who try
to help them.

Occasionally someone in the system — a volunteer,
judge, lawyer, policeman or jailer — is able to break
through the hardened, blind eyes of a juvenile offender
and help him or her see a world of forgiveness, hope, and
love. Persistent care and compassion sometimes get
through the built-up matter that blinds the soul's eyes.

Just a few years ago a self-described "gang banger,"
once hardened and tough, stood before our assembled

faculty. He spoke about his dreams of completing college and going on to law school. He moved us to tears as he talked about his gratitude for those who helped him see and opened his eyes to a bright world.

Isn't Jesus like that? We need a fresh encounter with a God of love and compassion. Like the juvenile offender, we too have cowered, flawed and failed behind a facade of success, cynicism or toughness. But Jesus, who came to cause the blind to see, disciplines us to cause us to cry for help, to repent and to know rebirth and revival. He causes us to recognize our own *con jobs*. We try to fool even those closest to us, but he knows we need sight.

I know. For once I too was blinded by pride and lust for prestige or honor. I groped for possessions, prestige — anything making me feel important. I failed miserably. But Jesus came, and through his discipline, my eyes were opened to the face of God and to his restoring love.

How about you? Have you allowed yourself to be judged by our holy and compassionate God?

— *L. Keith Whitney*

Reflections

1. "For we will all stand before God's judgment seat."
   — Romans 14:10

2. "Teach me knowledge and good judgment, for I believe in your commands."   — Psalm 119:66

3. "Life has no meaning except in terms of responsibility."   — Reinhold Niebuhr

4. God intends much of his judgment to correct and discipline us in this life.

5. "I have come to judge the world. I have come to give
    sight to the blind and to show those who think they
    see that they are blind."   — John 9:39 NLT

6. Loving demands judgment that chastens and calls us
    to repentance.

7. We need a fresh encounter with a God of love and
    compassion.

19

Trust and Obey

$\mathcal{O}$nce upon a time in a far distant land lived a strange character named Abram. His roots were as obscure as "Ur of the Chaldees," the place where he was living when he first learned to listen to the voice of God. Abram not only listened, he trusted God's promises and obeyed God's commands. At God's command, Abram left the people he knew, his position of power and many of his business interests. He did not yet know where God was taking him, but the adventure was new and exciting; trusting and obeying were easy.

Abraham, so named by God because he was man of faith and obedient servant, learned that trusting and obeying God would bring marvelous blessings. But God finally spoke the impossible, and Abraham laughed in disbelief. Yes, God had told Abraham and Sarah that he would bless all nations through the seed of Abraham. But how could Sarah, then in her nineties, bear the child? It was absurd. It was impossible. And, well, they just laughed right out loud. This man of faith could not believe God's promise.

Tell me again, Lord; I too so easily forget. Remind me that your promises are true and that you are the God of the impossible. Tell me the promises. Let me hear them again and again. Remind me as you did Abraham and Sarah, to whom you gave a child named Laughter (Isaac means "he laughs"). Perhaps then I too can learn to trust your promises. Yes, tell me again, Lord; I so easily forget.

Prophets, priests and even the ordinary people spoke often of God's Promised One, the Messiah. But captivity came. No Messiah. The nation itself was destroyed; walls crumbled. Still, no Messiah. And, again, at the most improbable time in the least likely of all places, God gave his Promised One to a peasant couple, who also simply trusted and obeyed. God's Messiah, the Promise Incarnate, God's Ultimate Surprise, came here to remind us just how much God loves us.

Hesed, a Hebrew word itself so obscure that its meaning is nearly impossible to define clearly, conveys the lovingkindness of God the Faithful and True. He is to be trusted and obeyed precisely because his love and promises to us rise to the feverish pitch of devotion. Promises connected to his Person preclude failure and make anything less than obedience absurd. *Show me again, Lord; I so easily forget you. Show me Jesus. Fix my eyes on him. Lest I forget the Person behind the promises.*

Just as suddenly as God's Promised One had appeared, he was gone again. Despised and rejected. Crucified. Resurrected to be sure. But gone. Ascended to the Father. And again came the promise of God. *He's coming back. In the same way, in a moment, the twinkling of an eye, he is coming again to claim his own, that where he is they may be also. Just as he had promised.*

Still, at times it seems so distant, so hard to believe. Daily we struggle just to cope with life's routine stresses. "Isn't it hard enough, Lord, just for me to keep up with the demands of my job and my family? I'm barely making it as it is, Lord."

Patiently he points to the Promised Prize. *Yes, Lord, tell me again; I so easily forget.* Trusting and obeying come incredibly hard to people like me who have such a hard time believing. I know *You* — the Person behind the Promise. I know You are faithful to the point of feverish devotion, that your grace and lovingkindness hold me.

But the prize seems so distant; my sins so great. I have a hard time trusting and obeying.

So I beg again, Lord. *Speak to me of your promises. Show me the Promised One. Keep ever before me the Prize. I so easily forget.* Help me live each moment, trusting that that which seems so distant, so improbable, will inevitably come to pass not because of who I am but precisely because of who you are and how immutable your promises are.

Lord, I want to laugh with the joy of surprise. I want to delight so much in your overwhelming surprise that you rename me Isaac, he who laughs. Give me the joy of trusting and obeying. Help me to rejoice always in you and your promises.

Tell me again, Lord; I so easily forget.

— *L. Keith Whitney*

Reflections

1. "*Hesed,* a Hebrew word itself so obscure that its meaning is nearly impossible to define clearly, conveys the lovingkindness of God the Faithful and True. He is to be trusted and obeyed precisely because his love and promises to us rise to the feverish pitch of devotion."

2. "Help me live each moment, trusting that that which seems so distant, so improbable, will inevitably come to pass not because of who I am but precisely because of who you are and how immutable your promises are."

3. "Give me the joy of trusting and obeying."

4. God desires obedience, motivated not by fear but by love and trust.

5. "In him our hearts rejoice, for we are trusting in his holy name."   — Psalm 33:21 TLB

6. "Though you do not see him, you trust him; and even now you are happy . . . ."   — 1 Peter 1:8 TLB

7. "In God We Trust."   — Motto on our money

20

Let God Be Right

*Y*ou and I are living in a society that has seen the triumph (at least temporarily) of relativism. We have moved from a correct position that acknowledges everyone's right to his or her own opinion — to the incorrect position that holds that everyone's opinion is equally right. In fact, just about the only "unpardonable sin" is to affirm that you are right and someone else is wrong on a particular issue. The new orthodoxy judges all of us to be somehow equally right. But honest, common-sense-thinking individuals know that is impossible.

Truth is not merely a subjective feeling. While beauty may be "in the eye of the beholder," truth most certainly is *not*. There is absolute, concrete, unalterable, eternal truth regarding many things, despite the protestations of the relativists. Our own age reminds me of those times recorded in the Bible when everyone did what was right in his or her own eyes. That is a pretty fair definition of anarchy, and anarchy is not only wrong, it is dangerous. Proverbs 14:12 says, "There is a way that seems right to a man, but in the end it leads to death."

The problem is that when a society refuses to recognize that universal truths exist, all morality becomes relative and simply a matter of opinion. And the result is lawlessness — as evidenced by the attitudes and actions of growing numbers of people in our nation. We don't have to look far to see dishonesty, crime, abuse, maliciousness, contempt and more, all of which are products of lawlessness.

Try to imagine a world where there is no natural law. It would be a world where birds fly sometimes and at other times cannot fly, where the sun rises sometimes and at other times does not, where heavy objects fall to the earth when dropped sometimes and at other times float. All of our scientific advancement has been predicated on *laws* that are constant, that never change. If the whole world operates on established natural laws, why would we suppose that we can establish *our own* moral laws?

It was God who laid down the natural laws, and it also was God who laid down all moral laws. Psalm 19:8 tells us: "The precepts of the Lord are right, giving joy to the heart. The commands of the Lord are radiant, giving light to the eyes." It follows that whenever the "precepts of the Lord" are ignored, there is no joy in the human heart. And it also follows that whenever the "commands of the Lord" are set aside, the light goes out of our eyes. We are blind.

Hosea concluded his prophecy this way: "Who is wise? He will realize these things. Who is discerning? He will understand them. The ways of the Lord are right; the righteous walk in them, but the rebellious stumble in them" (14:9). In many ways, the light has gone out for our society as a whole, and now it stumbles forward in the darkness. Hosea was telling the truth: The ways of the Lord are indeed right, and we will never discover another true and holy standard by which to live. Because *only God* is right.

In his theological discussion of the advantages of being a Jew, Paul said that the Jews had been entrusted with the very words of God. Then he said, "What if some did not have faith? Will their lack of faith nullify God's faithfulness? Not at all! Let God be true, and every man a liar" (Romans 3:3, 4).

Let God be true. Of course, God *is* true whether we *let him* be true or not. But we must let him be true *to us*. While you and I are unrighteous without God's forgiveness and justification, God himself is right — always right. What is more, he is the only standard for rightness. And if he is right, then his word is also right. That is why the psalmist wrote, "Your word is a lamp to my feet and a light for my path" (Psalm 119:105).

While philosophers, authors, moviemakers, politicians and poets struggle to find their individual truths, we do not have to flounder around in search of the right way to live or the right way to think or the right way to treat people. In this "politically correct" society, there is still only one way for Christians to walk. Jesus said, "I AM the way." We follow him, we live in him, we listen to his words and we obey.

In our daily lives, we must cut through the confusion and listen to only one voice. Let God be true. Let God be right. Let God's *word* be right. Resist the inclination to relegate holy Scripture to a distant time and a naive culture. And when we do that, joy will fill our hearts because of his precepts. Light will fill our eyes because of his commands.

— *Bill Henegar*

Reflections

1. "Let God be true, and every man a liar."
   — Romans 3:4

2. "Truth is not merely a subjective feeling."

3. "Your word is a lamp to my feet and a light for my path." — Psalm 119:105

4. "In our daily lives, we must cut through the confusion and listen to only one voice. Let God be true."

5. "There is a way that seems right to a man, but in the end it leads to death."   — Proverbs 14:12

6. "The Lord is near to all who call on him, to all who call on him in truth."   — Psalm 145:18

7. "The ways of the Lord are right; the righteous walk in them, but the rebellious stumble in them."

                                        — Hosea 14:9

Things That Are
PURE

21

Cry of the Human Heart

$\mathcal{O}$ne of the wonderful things about the Bible is that it identifies with us and speaks to our human condition. It is not a distant, esoteric document reserved only for theologians and philosophers. It is a message to the people.

Even the heroes of the Bible are ordinary folks with feet of clay — like us. David is a good example of that truth. He was a remarkable man: The Kingdom of the Israelites was at its height during his reign. But before he became a successful leader, he was a common shepherd. And even after he came to the throne, his human weaknesses remained and, in fact, were magnified.

David was a "man after God's own heart." What made him that was not his monumental righteousness, but his sincere heart. His sins, as it turned out, were great. But his heart was greater. Perhaps the most penetrating look into his soul is provided by his stirring Psalm 51. David's anguished words resonate with every true believer in his song.

You probably remember the story . . . It was a balmy spring evening as King David walked on the upper level of his palace. He looked out over the buildings that covered the hills of his beloved Jerusalem. But as he glanced down at a neighboring house, his eyes fell on a beautiful woman bathing. There in the warm, late-afternoon glow, he instantly encountered a powerful, physical stimulus and was faced with two choices. He could turn away and guard his heart, or he could give in and welcome impure thoughts. He chose the latter. His sensual passions proved stronger than his purity. In a short time, the impure thoughts had grown into evil deeds. First there was adultery, then there was murder.

How many times has that scenario been played out? Oh, not that *same exact* scenario. The circumstances may have been different. The temptation not the same. But whatever the situation, that age-old process has been repeated *billions* of times — both before David and on down to our own day. A person is confronted with a powerful stimulus (tantalized by power, popularity, possessions or some other temptation) and is faced with two choices. *Billions* of times, the wrong choice has been made.

We have all been there. We have all chosen disastrously — we have fallen. That is why Psalm 51 has such a familiar ring to it. It is not only David's song. It is *our song*. It is the cry of the human heart. With David we confess, "I know my transgressions, and my sin is always before me. Against you, you only, have I sinned and done what is evil in your sight . . . ."

Like the shepherd-king of Israel, we cry, "Have mercy on me, O God, according to your unfailing love . . . blot out my transgressions. Wash away all my iniquity and cleanse me from my sin." But perhaps David's key words are squarely in the center of the song. They form a fervent prayer that we all must share: "Create in me a pure heart, O God," he said, "and renew a steadfast spirit within me."

In every age, men and women have turned away from God. We are no different. This, then, has been and ever will be the cry of the human heart: "My sin is always before me . . . create in me a pure heart."

Also in every age, people have sought to find God and salvation through the practice of religious works. But we must know, as did David, that it is impossible to find God through works. No matter what David did, his "sin was always before" him. He correctly identified how to come to God: "Create in me a pure heart." God is the Creator. Only he can create a pure heart.

However, God does not create a pure heart in us and then turn us loose to be on our own. We must come to him daily, hourly, with the same plea: "Create in me a pure heart." If that is the cry of MY human heart, I believe God hears my plea with every beat of my physical heart. That is my desire — that with every pulse, my unconscious prayer calls for God to make my heart fresh and pure.

It is crucially important to not thwart God's creation by crowding our heart with impurities. Can I truly ask him for a pure heart if I am cramming it with hate or greed or lust faster than he can make it pure? I must *cooperate* with his creation by immediately giving my heart to him as I encounter temptations. "Take the taste of that desire from my mouth," I must pray.

Here is a tremendously encouraging thought: *God answers the cry of the human heart.* As we cry, "O God, create in me a pure heart," he does exactly that. And he does it not from a distance, but from the inside. Which is where he has placed his Holy Spirit.

— *Bill Henegar*

Reflections

1. "Breathe on me, Breath of God, until my heart is pure, Until my will is one with Thine, to do and to endure."   — Edwin Hatch

2. "Create in me a pure heart, O God, and renew a steadfast spirit within me."   — Psalm 51:10

3. "Can I truly ask [God] for a pure heart if I am cramming it with hate or greed or lust faster than he can make it pure?"

4. "Blessed are the pure in heart, for they will see God."
— Matthew 5:8

5. "I praise Thee, Lord, for cleansing me from sin; Fulfill Thy Word and make me pure within. Fill me with fire, where once I burned with shame; Grant my desire to magnify Thy name."   — J. Edwin Orr

6. "God answers the cry of the human heart."

7. "But if we walk in the light, as he is in the light, we have fellowship with one another, and the blood of Jesus, his Son, purifies us from every sin."
— 1 John 1:7

22

Keep Yourself Pure?

*T*he old mentor admonished the young preacher to "not share in the sins of others." He also advised him to do something that sounds incredibly old-fashioned to us today. "Keep yourself pure," Paul told Timothy (1 Timothy 5:22).

Many people, perhaps even we ourselves, react to such advice with amused disregard. Keep yourself pure? It sounds so Victorian, so quaint, so naive. Maybe that was a reasonable goal for some bygone society, or some present backwater culture. But where you and I live, it is considered hopelessly ridiculous. Watch nearly any television show; go to nearly any motion picture. Everyone knows the world just isn't like that anymore. Such advice, if useful at all, is good only for preachers and other "holy" people. Right?

The aged apostle John, near the end of his life, seemed to look deep into the future, to that Day of Glory when Jesus comes for his people. And John wrote: "Dear friends, now we are children of God, and what we will be has not yet been made known. But we know that when he appears, we shall be like him, for we shall see him as he is." What an electrifying thought! What an extraordinary vision! We shall see him as he is!

But John was not finished. He continued, "Everyone who has this hope in him purifies himself, just as he is pure" (1 John 3:3). Everyone? Yes, everyone who has that wonderful hope "purifies himself." Because the reigning Jesus is absolutely pure, and those who wait for his appearance prepare themselves to be like their Lord.

Long ago, England's Charlotte Elliott penned some verses that have helped to turn countless hearts toward Christ. "Just as I am!" she wrote, "without one plea, But that Thy blood was shed for me." Truer words have never been written. The closing words of each stanza are the same: "O Lamb of God, I come! I come!"

Jesus bids us come just as we are. But he *commands us* to not remain as we are! Paul's benediction for the Thessalonian Christians went like this: "May he strengthen your hearts so that you will be blameless and holy in the presence of our God and Father when our Lord Jesus comes with all his holy ones" (1 Thessalonians 3:13). Picture this: Jesus, the *Holy* One, comes to receive us. With him are all his *holy* ones. Suddenly we stand in the presence of the *Holy* God. Do we imagine we will be able to stand in that assemblage as the only *unholy* ones?

The writer of the Book of Hebrews explains the process well: "Our fathers disciplined us for a little while as they thought best; but God disciplines us for our good, that we may share in his holiness" (Hebrews 12:10). We are not becoming more and more tainted or corrupt. We are not even staying the same. We are becoming more and more pure. God sees to it — unless we remove ourselves from beneath his discipline.

Not only does God discipline us, but we also have an urgent agenda ourselves. We are called to participate in holiness. "Make every effort to live in peace with all men and to be holy," the writer finally says (Hebrews 12:14). God changes us, makes us pure and holy. But as John told us, we must purify *ourselves*. And as Paul told Timothy, we must *keep* ourselves pure.

"Make every effort to live in peace with all men and to be holy," the writer said. Then he concluded, "without holiness no one will see the Lord." If someone asks you if you are pure, or if you are godly, or if you are holy, what do you say? Do you say, "No" or "I hope so"? Remember, "without holiness *no one will see the Lord.*" We have no choice in this matter. We *must* be holy. We *must* live a pure life.

What does it mean to live a pure life? It certainly does not mean to live a perfect life — because only our Lord was capable of that. All those archaic-sounding words — *pure, holy, godly* — relate to God. Only God is truly pure, holy, godly. But if we are children of God, we will try to be like him . . . in the same way we tried to be like our human parents when we were children. We were imperfect little replicas of our parents, trying desperately to talk like them, walk like them, be like them. And one day we looked into the mirror with shock and saw our parents in us!

So we must be about the business of imitating our Father in heaven. It is impossible to keep impure thoughts and motives from entering our minds, but we can immediately cast them out. We cannot completely keep from sinning, but we can reject those sins, renounce them as unholy. We can keep submitting to the discipline of the God who loves us.

We can struggle daily to keep ourselves pure. Because the Lord is coming.

— *Bill Henegar*

Reflections

1. "More purity give me, More strength to o'ercome,
   More freedom from earthstains,
   More longings for home;
   More fit for the kingdom, More useful I'd be,
   More blessed and holy, More, Savior, like Thee."
   — Philip B. Bliss

2. "So we must be about the business of imitating our Father in heaven."

3. "Everyone who has this hope in him purifies himself, just as he is pure."   — 1 John 3:3

4. "We cannot completely keep from sinning, but we can reject those sins, renounce them as unholy."

5. "Just as I am! without one plea,
   But that Thy blood was shed for me,
   And that Thou bidd'st me come to Thee,
   O Lamb of God I come! I come!"
                                              — Charlotte Elliott

6. "May he strengthen your hearts so that you will be blameless and holy in the presence of our God and Father when our Lord Jesus comes with all his holy ones."   — 1 Thessalonians 3:13

7. "Make every effort to live in peace with all men and to be holy."   — Hebrews 12:14

23

Developing Childlike Lives

One of the revolutionary concepts that Jesus introduced into the world is expressed in Matthew 18:1-5: "At that time the disciples came to Jesus and asked, 'Who is the greatest in the kingdom of heaven?' He called a little child and had him stand among them. And he said: 'I tell you the truth, unless you change and become like little children, you will never enter the kingdom of heaven. Therefore, whoever humbles himself like this child is the greatest in the kingdom of heaven. And whoever welcomes a little child like this in my name welcomes me.'"

In this renowned passage, two verbs are used that are significant: "change" and "become." Some translations use "turn" for "change." These verbs are a great commentary on each of us. We are **not** like little children. We are often egotistical, proud, self-serving and hardened. Little children are usually none of these. Jesus wants us to become like little children.

The people listening to Jesus, even his own apostles, were going the wrong way: they were told to "turn" or "change." Furthermore, Jesus said, "whosoever humbles himself like this child is the greatest in the kingdom of heaven." What a challenge! What a difference this is to the way the world thinks. In the world, one of the key ideas is to "succeed," and success frequently is dependent not upon the forgetting of self, but rather on the "selling" of self.

Jesus was a revolutionary person. His life did not always correspond to the ways and values of the people of his day. Whereas John the Baptist lived a strict, ascetic life and was accused of having a demon, Jesus was accused of being a glutton and a drunkard; and a friend of tax collectors and sinners (Luke 7:33-34). Jesus was not afraid to confront people where they were and challenge their sinful and confusing rules about life.

One of the most revolutionary statements that Jesus made comes from Matthew 18:1-5, which is quoted above. In our world, greatness often means power and control over others. Riches and fame are often identified with success. Many would never identify humility as a symbol of greatness. But, Jesus clearly states that "the way **up** is frequently **down**." Until we can fall on our knees and worship God, we cannot know the real meaning of greatness.

Jesus is the Son of God. Under his feet, God has placed everything in the world and beyond the world (see Ephesians 1:23). He is superior to all of the kings of all the earth. When people walked into the throne rooms of the great kings, they fell on their faces. Often, if they were not invited in by the king, he would hold out his scepter to them. If he did not want to see them, he would have them put to death (see Esther 4:11). Jesus was not that way. He wants us in his presence. He declared that "all authority in heaven and on earth has been given to me" (Matthew 28:18). He wants us to be subject to him, just as little children are subject to authority.

Yet, this pilgrim to Bethlehem, Jesus, said that he did not come "to be served, but rather to serve, and to give his life as a ransom for many" (Matthew 20:28). In this statement of Jesus that we must become as little children, he is telling us that the way "up" is "down," down on our knees. We must humble ourselves and become as little children if we want to become the greatest in the kingdom of heaven.

Why should we want to "become as little children"? After all, do we not spend all of our lives trying to "grow up," become mature and develop into adults? Well, Jesus was certainly not talking about our "becoming as little children" in a physical way. Jesus was indicating that children have characteristics that adults do not have. It is in **this** way that Jesus wants us to become as little children.

Little children are more humble than we adults are. Although they have a desire to please themselves, as all of us have, they do not always think of promoting themselves to the expense of other people. Competition in the adult world includes our desire to "outdo" the other person, to become greater than other people. Children do not generally think in this way.

Little children tend to be more forgiving than we adults are. It seems that the older and more set in our ways we become, the more unforgiving we tend to become. Children generally do not hold grudges as long as we adults do. Certainly a child will react and respond to others' actions toward them; but they are more willing to forgive sooner than many of us are.

Jesus is very insistent that we humble ourselves and become as little children. What a great world it would be if we could all have childlike spirits! Jesus said that those who become as little children will be "the greatest in the kingdom of heaven" (Matthew 18:4).

— *Morris M. Womack*

Reflections

1. In what ways is the "new birth" (John 3:3-5) related to our becoming "like little children?" (see Matthew 18:1-5)

2. How does Jesus' declaration that we should "become like little children" indicate that Jesus was revolutionary in his teaching?

3. "How great is the love the Father has lavished on us, that we should be called children of God. And that is what we are! . . . Dear friends, now we are the children of God."   — 1 John 3:1-3

4. "Children are God's apostles, day by day
   Sent forth to preach of love, and hope, and peace."
                                          — James Russell Lowell

5. "Give a little love to a child, and you get a great deal back."   — John Ruskin

6. "Blessed be childhood, which brings down something of heaven into the midst of our rough earthliness."
                                          — Frederic Amiel

7. The way we train our children today will determine what the home, the church, and the world will be tomorrow.

24

To Know Jesus My Lord

$\mathcal{M}$ichael Card is a well-known songwriter and singer of contemporary Christian music. I believe he is unique among today's artists because he is both a devoted student of the Word of God, with a graduate degree in biblical studies, and a gifted artist. As such, he is concerned with the music but also the integrity of the lyrics. Many of his songs touch my heart. One very simple song has special meaning to me. It is entitled, "Jesus, Let Us Come to Know You." He writes:

Jesus, let us
Come to know you.
Let us see you
Face to face.
Touch us; hold us.
Use us; mold us.
Only let us
Live in you.

Jesus, draw us,
Ever nearer;
Hold us in your
Loving arms.
Wrap us in your
Gentle presence;
And when the end comes,
Bring us home.

Why is it so important to come to know Jesus as Lord and Savior? Why is it so critical to our spiritual survival and growth to think about him? Who is Jesus? What did he come to this Earth to do? Did he have to come? Just how can I come to know him anyway? Questions. We have so many questions.

First, in order for us to know who we really are ourselves, we have to understand Jesus. He is the real thing, the pattern after whose image we were made. The Christian's worldview begins with the biblical assertion that man is a moral creature made in the very image of God. But just what does the Bible mean by the "image" of God? Only by seeing Jesus, God incarnate, Word become flesh, can we begin to comprehend what we were intended to be. Only in Jesus do we see what the image of God in human form is like.

A second difficulty we experience is in trying to understand the words of the Father. If we are to believe the biblical accounts, then we are compelled to see God's word as both moral absolutes resting on the very character of God himself and, at the same time, as loving instructions of the Father directing the growth and development of his children. But words without earthly or even earthy illustration are difficult for us. Few of us understand deep philosophical arguments about man's moral dilemma or about existentialism or about any other theological concept. We cannot even grasp God's love or anyone's love until it has skin on it. It is only when we see Jesus in life and in death that we understand all of theology that really matters: God is love.

Finally, we learn best by modeling behavior we admire, behavior we see as commendable and worthy. We begin to understand that our own lives are filled with fear, failure, despair, and guilt. But seeing Jesus and witnessing his humility and compassionate service, I begin to understand my own selfishness and indifference, the true opposite of love. In the life of Jesus, the God who serves, I find a mentor who demonstrates life as it was meant to be lived by all God's children.

As I reflect on his life and sacrificial death, I am forced to consider what it was like for the God over all creation to come to this speck of a place, to dwell with selfish sinners who had forsaken the character of God for pitiful passions of the flesh and to demonstrate his love for us even as we continued to pursue our own selfish dreams and schemes. The cross of Jesus shows us both the love of God and the importance of man. He suffered willingly, knowing that his suffering was for you and me. He suffered not only the humiliation of the cross but also the indignity of human incarnation. We were the child lost in the night; we were the infants struggling for sight. We were the lame, the lonely, in despair and death; we were the thieves, the middle-cross dwellers, in search of meaning beyond the grave. We still are . . . until he comes to show us the way, the truth and the life.

I want to know Jesus. For to know Jesus is to know that life, my life and yours, matters to God. To know Jesus is to know love has skin on it. To know him is to understand that God wants all his children to live with grace, compassion and love. *"Jesus, let us come to know you."*

— *L. Keith Whitney*

Reflections

1. "I want to know Christ and the power of his resurrection and the fellowship of sharing in his sufferings, becoming like him in his death, and so, somehow, to attain to the resurrection from the dead."
   — Philippians 3:10

2. We really do not grasp love until it has skin on it.

3. Through his life and his death on the cross, Jesus is able to offer us a glimpse of God and to confirm the importance of man.

4. To know Jesus is to know that life, my life also, matters to God.

5. "Jesus, draw us ever nearer; hold us in your loving arms. Wrap us in your gentle presence; and when the end comes, bring us home."   — Michael Card

6. "But our citizenship is in heaven. And we eagerly await a Savior from there, the Lord Jesus Christ . . . ."
                                        — Philippians 3:20

7. "And my God will meet all your needs according his glorious riches in Christ Jesus." — Philippians 4:19

25

Made Holy by His Spirit

*A*ccording to the text of God's word, the very Spirit of God indwells the Christian individually (See Romans 8:9 and 11, for example). In fact, the body of the Christian is said to be the temple of the Spirit (1 Corinthians 6:19). The Spirit remains in the Christian and makes his home there, according to the apostle John (1 John 3:24; 4:13). Yet, I frequently sing with great zeal, "Spirit of the Living God, fall afresh on me," for I feel anything but his presence. Perhaps I am just experiencing the truth of the old East Texas expression, "If you lay down with dogs, you'll pick up fleas." My life has gone to the dogs sometimes, and I think I feel the itch.

We are like the eagle, equipped by God for flight, able to soar above all the disgusting garbage of life, but we frequently act confused. We seem to have encountered chickens or some other bird that prefers the ground and its produce. Like orphaned birds who first see a bird of another species and identify with it, we identify with these earthbound creatures. The imprint left in our minds is all wrong. Hunting and pecking in the dirt were never intended for us. Searching for love in back seats or dark hotels, in all the wrong places, results from the world's imprint. The problem is that we were created to soar. We are created in the image of God with space awaiting his Spirit to indwell us. We can never be satisfied or happy with the crumbs thrown to us, for we are inevitably longing for more. We were created to find our rest in God; we are forever hungering and thirsting for more unless filled with his presence in us.

I grew up around quail. If you have ever been around quail, you understand what weird birds they are. They are capable of flight, but they usually prefer running on the ground instead. It is only when they conclude that "their number is up," that they start flying. Otherwise, they stay on the ground and run. The vast majority of us spend our lives in frantic pursuit of earthly goals that, when they are achieved, often leave us unfulfilled and still running.

With Thomas à Kempis, I say, "Set me free from evil passions, and heal my heart of all inordinate affections; that being inwardly cured and thoroughly cleansed, I may be made fit to love, courageous to suffer, steady to persevere." Isn't that a wonderful prayer? Do you also feel the need to be cleansed of the soil left by running in earthy, worldly pursuits? Would you be pure in heart and mind again and free to soar?

The Holy Spirit washes us, sanctifies us and justifies us in the name of the Lord Jesus Christ (1 Corinthians 6:11). His Spirit within us purifies us so that we can live as we were intended to live — to the praise of his glorious grace. This body is not meant for sexual immorality or any earthbound, selfish pursuit. We are the dwelling place of God's Spirit and challenged to live honoring God with our bodies. The Father wants us to soar like eagles.

Plato reportedly said, "We ought to fly away from Earth to heaven as quickly as we can; and to fly away is to become like God, as far as this is possible; and to become like him is to become holy, just and wise." And, lest you believe there is no biblical sentiment like Plato's words, listen to a sampling of verses in 1 John 4:

Verse 13, "We know that we live in him and he in us, because he has given us his Spirit."

Verse 16b, "God is love. *Whoever lives in love lives in*

God, and God in him. In this way, love is made complete among us so that we will have confidence on the day of judgment, because *in this world we are like him."*

So, we were created to be like God, to soar above it all. Why, then, are we earthbound and unable to fly? I submit it is because we are caught in a myriad of selfish attachments. Little things really. Like Jonathan Swift's Gulliver, tied with thousands of little strings anchored to the ground with tiny pegs, we are earthbound, tied by thousands of little selfish attachments. For some of us, the tie lies in our possessions. Others are tied to earth by lust or greed or power. But whether it be a steel cable or thousands of delicate threads that hold earthbound birds, "it matters not, if it really holds us fast; for, until the cord be broken, the bird cannot fly" (Saint John of the Cross).

What can break the attachments? What can cleanse us and free us? With Thomas à Kempis, pray for the Spirit of the Living God to heal our hearts of earthly attachments and affections; that being cured and cleansed thoroughly by his Spirit, you may be made fit to love, courageous to soar, steady to persevere. *Cleanse me and make me holy by your Spirit, O Lord God Almighty.*

— *L. Keith Whitney*

Reflections

1. "Do you not know that your body is a temple of the Holy Spirit, who is in you, whom you have received from God?" — 1 Corinthians 6:19

2. "We know that we live in him and he in us, because he has given us his Spirit." — 1 John 4:13

3. "Set me free from evil passions, and heal my heart of all inordinate affections; that being inwardly cured

and thoroughly cleansed, I may be made fit to love, courageous to suffer, steady to persevere."

— Thomas à Kempis

4. "The vast majority of us spend our lives in frantic pursuit of earthly goals that, when they are achieved, often leave us unfulfilled and still running."

5. "We are created in the image of God with space awaiting his Spirit to indwell us."

6. "God is love. Whoever lives in love lives in God, and God in him."   — 1 John 4:16b

7. "But you were washed, you were sanctified, you were justified in the name of the Lord Jesus Christ and by the Spirit of our God."   — 1 Corinthians 6:11b

26

On Purity: "True Love Waits"

*T*here is a certain degree of hypocrisy in me, at least in my decision to write this encouragement to parents and youth. Perhaps nothing has moved me more in the past few years than the beauty of the "True Love Waits" programs instituted by several churches in America. In most of these programs, sons and daughters pledge their purity until marriage. A ring is given at a special ceremony of commitment. This ring is to be removed by the young person's spouse at some point during their marriage ceremony or just prior to the sexual union of the new husband and wife. So why do I feel like a hypocrite?

Well, the truth is that my wife should be writing this article. While I have admired the program instituted at many churches, my children have not attended a church with such a program. Instead, I have been blessed by a wonderful wife who has communicated the beauty and purity of sex within marriage to our daughters. Since I do not have a son, I have been able to pass the proverbial buck to my wife. In embarrassment, I dedicate this article to my two daughters for whom I have both great love and respect.

In the movies and in the locker rooms in which I have grown up, sex was made out to be something dirty. My parents never spoke of such matters at all. Today people seem to accept sexual relationships as more natural, but it still seems to be rather coarse or dirty. Pornographic materials abound. Sex is often crude and lustful. Using another for our own pleasure is in fashion. Sex is touted as a recreational participation for everyone, married or not. The Internet webs and VCR's of America are full of vulgar images engaged in every act imaginable. Innocence is lost. Gone are the beauty and purity of sex within marriage.

Unfortunately, we Christians have let the world define what sex means. We have allowed the world to degrade the beauty and meaning of the covenant relationship of one man with one woman. We have too frequently remained silent, ashamed of God's wonderful gift; or worse, we have bought into the world's definitions. We proclaim that sex within marriage is good, while we secretly believe that sex is nasty, dirty and enjoyable only in rebellion to God.

When we make sex a hidden and secretive adult pleasure, our children may be encouraged to explore the thrills as they reach for adulthood. When we view sex as part of God's marvelous plan, we see it as God's gift of ultimate intimacy for a man and woman who are committed to one another in the most special way possible. Pure eyes see a man joined, at-one-with his wife. Purity encourages us to recognize the incredible beauty of two hearts so linked, two lives so together, that we literally come to know the other's body as well as our own. Pure hearts know that "making love" is not some cheap act for the back seat of a car. Purity demands that we not cheapen the spiritual significance of sexual union by viewing it as merely a biological act or cheap thrill.

Stop a moment and reflect about your own marriage and your relationship with your spouse. Whether that marriage took place long ago or remains a dream for your future, realize that sex is a God-given sacrament. During sexual intercourse, we are able to participate momentarily in a symbolic spiritual union. Husband and wife know the special sense of bliss that comes through sexual intimacy with one other person.

In Christ we are at-one-with God. His very spirit indwells us. In marriage God calls us into union with another person. Two become spiritually one. Sex unites in a way that only the pure understand. Intimacy's secrets are delightful, allowing two persons to communicate the depth of their love in unique ways reserved only for the two of them. Intimacy's secrets may make no sense to other persons. The depth of the resulting relationship defies description. Only the initiate understands.

True loves waits for marriage. And the special intimacy of married love is worth the wait. Purity, God's way, has truly mysterious rewards. The mystery is fully revealed only to the pure who participate in marriage as God designed it. I encourage all, young and old, never-marrieds and singles-again, to wait. So does the Creator; he also encourages us to wait. *True love* waits.

— *L. Keith Whitney*

Reflections

1. "Purity demands that we not cheapen the spiritual significance of sexual union by viewing it as merely a biological act or cheap thrill."

2. "Purity encourages us to recognize the incredible beauty of two hearts so linked, two lives so together, that we literally come to know the other's body as well as our own."

3. "For this reason a man will leave his father and mother and be united to his wife, and the two will become one flesh." — Ephesians 5:31

4. "But a man who commits adultery lacks judgment; whoever does so destroys himself." — Proverbs 6:32

5. "Ask yourself not if this or that is expedient, but if it is right."   — Alan Paton

6. "There is no more lovely, friendly, and charming relationship, communion, or company than a good marriage."   — Martin Luther

7. "Marriage is our last, best chance to grow up."
                                    — Joseph Barth

27

This Is Pure Religion

*I*f our religion is not pure, then our lives will not be pure. If we want to think on the right things, we need to know what these right things are. James makes an astonishing statement as he writes about pure living. "Religion that God our Father accepts as pure and faultless is this: to look after orphans and widows in their distress and to keep oneself from being polluted by the world" (James 1:27).

This statement from James does not harmonize with much of the thinking of our current world. From looking at our society, one might think that pure religion is represented by lavish and ornate church buildings; or that pure religion might involve deeply meaningful rituals to be carried out in those buildings. We might be led to believe that if we have very spiritual and beautifully planned worship services, our religion qualifies as pure. So many things make up our worship activities today. So we spend our time and money making sure that everything looks and sounds right in the sight of God. James does not seem to be saying that all of these things are necessarily wrong; he is simply saying that many of us have missed the point on what **pure religion** really is. We must not let the form take the place of the real thing.

But, why does James single out "orphans and widows in their distress" as one of the two ingredients of "religion that God our Father accepts"? Consider for a moment the plight of widows and orphans. They really are two groups of people who are often destitute and with no means of caring for themselves. This was especially true in biblical days. A widow in Jesus' day was truly someone to sympathize with. She had lost her means of livelihood and physical support. There were few jobs that a widow could find as a means of caring for needs. She had lost the companionship of her husband; she was alone; many had not the time nor the inclination to spend time with a widow. Orphans were in somewhat the same state of being. They have lost their parents, their home and any means of being cared for, and they often tended to be destitute. These two groups of needy people — widows and orphans — were actually forsaken by the mainstream of society. Pure religion is, therefore, truly expressed in caring for these people.

What does it mean to *"look after* orphans and widows *in their distress"*? Earlier translations used the term "visit" to describe this action. The Greek verb *episkopeo* literally means to care for, watch over. It carries with it the idea of extending acts of kindness. Those who are "down and out," as orphans and widows often are, will be greatly strengthened and encouraged when someone extends an act of kindness, or cares for them. Just recently, I was called to the home of a dear Christian widow, who was undergoing panic stress. I sat with her for quite some time, listened to her concerns, gave very little advice but gave her my ear. This was what she needed.

Widows and orphans often fall into a category of people who can give little in return for the assistance we give. This is truly the practice of the *agape* type of love. When we "look after" them, we will not be expecting anything in return. This practice of Christian love is getting to the very heart of what it means to be a servant of our fellow beings.

In both the Old and New Testaments, caring for

those who are unable to "return the favor" is made a noble deed. Job, for example, spoke of his caring for the homeless or helping those in need as one of the evidences of his own righteous behavior (see Job 31). David spoke of being a "father to the fatherless, a defender of widows" as one of the ways of singing praise to God (Psalm 68:5ff.). Because God is a defender of "the cause of the fatherless and the widow" (Deuteronomy 10:18), and the law warned against taking advantage of the widow (Exodus 22:22). So important was the widow in the early church that there seems to have been a special group of widows. Paul admonishes, "Give proper recognition to those widows who are really in need" (1 Timothy 5:4); and "No widow may be put on the list of widows unless" certain qualifications are in place (1 Timothy 5:9ff.). So, pure religion, in truth, involves caring for widows and orphans and any who are truly less fortunate than we.

— *Morris M. Womack*

Reflections

1. Why is the following true? "Religion that God our Father accepts as pure and faultless is this: to look after orphans and widows in their distress and to keep oneself from being polluted by the world" (James 1:27).

2. "Nothing is so fatal to religion as indifference."
                                                        — Edward Burke

3. "Men will wrangle for religion, write for it, die for it; anything but live for it."
                                                        — Charles Caleb Cotton

4. Why do you think God made "caring for widows and orphans" descriptive symbols for religion?

5. Consider this statement: Caring for those who are unable to "return the favor" is a noble deed.

6. In what ways are caring for orphans and widows related to Jesus' admonishment to us to wash one another's feet? (see John 13:1-17).

7. "Give proper recognition to those widows who are really in need. But if a widow has children or grand-children, these should learn first of all to put their religion in practice by caring for their family and so repaying their parents and grandparents, for this is pleasing to God."   — 1 Timothy 5:3-4

Things That Are
LOVELY

28

The Beauty of the World Is Ours

The Psalmist must have been filled with awe as he exclaimed: "The heavens declare the glory of God; the skies proclaim the work of his hands. Day after day they pour forth speech; night after night they display knowledge. There is no speech or language where their voice is not heard. Their voice goes out into all the earth, their words to the ends of the world" (Psalm 19:1-4). Their silent testimony declares the presence of the Creator.

As I write, I am sitting in the midst of the towering Ponderosa and Piñon pine trees in the smog-free atmosphere of Big Bear, California. For miles around, the wonders of God's beautiful world are flashing their beauties to all who pass by.

It is no accident that God's creation is beautiful. Solomon wrote that God "has made everything beautiful in its time" (Ecclesiastes 3:11). Jesus punctuated the beauty of God's world when he said: "See how the lilies of the field grow. They do not labor or spin. Yet I tell you that Solomon in all his splendor was not dressed like one of these" (Matthew 6:28-29). The beauty of the world has been marred only by the abuse mankind has foisted upon it.

The striking contrasts exhibited in the beauty of the world are testimony to the existence of an all-powerful Creator. How can the breathtaking snow-capped peaks of

Switzerland be compared with the towering giant red-
woods of northwestern California? Or how can the
glimmering ice-peaked mountains of Alaska be compared
with the unique beauty of the sprawling deserts of
Arizona? The beauty of the world is a vivid testimony to
the existence of a supernatural Creator. But, what does
this say to us, his creatures?

It demonstrates the matchless love of God. This
world with all of its beauty was created as a home for
mankind. Consider the Garden of Eden in its pristine
purity. Before sin corrupted the hearts of Adam and Eve,
the Garden of Eden was a literal paradise. Even the Tree
of Knowledge of Good and Evil was "pleasing to the eye"
(Genesis 3:3). Yet even after sin corrupted the world,
God's beauty is still seen through what he created. We
enjoy beauty because of the enormous love of God.

**The beauty of the world demonstrates how beautiful
heaven must be.** When Jesus left his disciples, he had
promised that "in my Father's house are many rooms; if
it were not so, I would have told you. I am going there to
prepare a place for you" (John 14:2). Paul and John both
saw visions of the beauty of God's heaven. Surely it was
Paul who looked beyond and "heard inexpressible
things" (2 Corinthians 12:5). And, who can comprehend the majesty of the eternal city described by John in
his revelation from Christ himself? (see Revelation 21:1-
5). Because the human mind cannot comprehend the
beauty of the eternal, John described his vision in
human terms — the river of water, the street of gold, the
walls and gates made of the most beautiful of stones. We
often sing a song, "How beautiful heaven must be."

**The beauty of the world demonstrates how beautiful
God must be.** I am not speaking of physical beauty, for
God is not physical. The religious leader Anselm, many
years ago, gave seven great proofs for the existence of
God. He argued that everything is beautiful in comparison to something more beautiful than itself. Following
this logic, you could go back only so far until you reach

the ultimate beauty. And that ultimate beauty, reasoned Anselm, was God. Just as an artist needs a sense of beauty to create a beautiful masterpiece, even more does the beauty of the world need a Creator with a sense of beauty.

We live in a beautiful world. We owe it to our Creator to nurture and care for God's creation. God placed Adam in the Garden of Eden "to work it and take care of it" (Genesis 2:15). How much more is it our responsibility and privilege to take care of and adorn our beautiful world? Many of us have not been very good providers for God's creation. We have polluted the air and the water; we have scattered our trash all across our land. Let us resolve to take back our responsibility to dress and adorn the world. God has built into his creation an amazing recovery system. If we will cooperate with him, much of the lost beauty will be restored.

— *Morris M. Womack*

Reflections

1. "The heavens declare the glory of God, the skies proclaim the work of his hands."   —Psalm 19:1

2. What did David mean when he wrote, "There is no speech or language where their voice is not heard. Their voice goes into all the earth, their words to the ends of the world"? (see Psalm 19:3-4)

3. "For the beauty of the earth,
   For the beauty of the skies,
   For the love which from our birth
   Over and around us lies:
   Lord, of all, to thee we raise
   This our sacrifice of praise."   — Folliot S. Pierpoint

4. "The spacious firmament on high,
    With all the blue, ethereal sky,
    And spangled heavens, a shining frame,
    Their great Original proclaim:
    Th' unwearied sun from day to day
    Does his Creator's power display,
    And publishes to every land
    The work of an almighty hand." — Joseph Addison

5. "This world, after all our science and sciences, is still
    a miracle: wonderful, inscrutable, magical and more,
    to whosoever will think of it."   —Thomas Carlyle

6. "See how the lilies of the field grow. They do not labor
    nor spin. Yet I tell you that Solomon in all his splen-
    dor was not dressed like one of these."
                                        —Matthew 6:28, 29

7. God has built into his creation an amazing recovery
    system. If we cooperate with Him, much of the lost
    beauty can be restored. What can I do?

29

Heaven: Most Beautiful and Majestic Castle of All

As we drove the route through Mittenwald, Bavaria, close to the Austrian frontier, a region of lofty alpine peaks, glacial lakes and picturesque villages, we thought we were approaching heaven itself. Then, we looked up to see the fairy-tale castle of Neuschwanstein, one of the world's most fantastic edifices, neo-Romanesque in style, perched on the highest of rocks above us. Designed by the theater painter C. Jank, conceived by the eccentric Bavarian King Ludwig II, it had taken 17 years to complete (1869-1886). Its name means "new swan's rock" and refers to the beautiful lake below, the Schwansee, with its many swans. As we hiked up the trail to the castle, I thought we were approaching the gates of heaven itself. It was awesome!

But then I thought of crazy King Ludwig and the verse in Matthew 6, where Jesus reminds us, "Where your treasure is, there will your heart be also." Ludwig also ordered the construction of a copy of Versailles, Herrenchiemsee castle, on an isle in the lake of Chiemsee. Neglecting his duties of state and devoting more and more time and money to his obsessions, Ludwig was eventually declared insane and shortly thereafter found drowned in the Sharnberger See. Officially, it was declared a suicide, but many suspect it was foul play. Ludwig had lived his life in the selfish pursuit of castles in the air. His heart was in the stone of his castle walls. It would forever be.

Have you ever given any thought to the reality of heaven? Have you ever wondered about the surpassing glory of heaven and the marvelously unspeakable beauty beyond description which awaits us there? A.W. Tozer said of heaven,

> *To regain her lost power, the church must see heaven opened and have a transforming vision of God. . . . The God we must learn to know is the Majesty in the heavens. . . ."*

Why? Well, as I read the description of heaven written by John in Revelation 21:9-11, I am struck by the blinding brilliance of heaven. God's glory fills heaven with a dazzling splendor above any Spielberg special effect.

Deep within each of us beats a heart longing for heaven and eternity. Heaven is not a place of harps and clouds; instead, it is a place beyond description, exciting, wonderful and joyful! Heaven multiplies joy in our lives, for the happiest persons are those who have learned to live lives focused on Jesus and his eternal glory. Joyful are those with heads in heaven, viewing the majestic glory of God, as they walk the rugged terrain of this world.

False is the old saying, "He's so heavenly minded, he's no earthly good." In fact, only those who are heavenly minded are fit for this life, this earth. Only with a true vision of heaven burning constantly in our mind's eye can we see with eternal perspective. Only with eternity in view, the surpassing beauty of heaven itself filling our eyes, can we truly understand what is valuable. Only as God reveals true beauty to us can we learn to live for eternity. We will not spend our life as this generation's crazy King Ludwig. No, as Jim Elliot the missionary and martyr is quoted as saying, "One life to live, will soon be past. Only what's done for Christ will last."

You see, perspective is everything. The higher you are, the better you see.

I recently heard a story that illustrates the point about perspective well. A young man who had served God as a minister and guide to others learned he had a terrible cancer. It was inoperable. He was told that he would die fairly quickly. Depression overwhelmed him. Suddenly, he was destroyed by the reality of his impending death.

In hopes that a trip to the mountains he loved so much would cheer him and break the hold depression had on him, his wife planned a relatively easy hike. As they hiked toward a ranger's cabin near a beautiful lake, most in the party were struck by the sheer beauty of it all. The crystal lake reflected the majestic Cascades in the background. The verdant forest, the lake, the mountains and the sky formed a masterpiece beyond compare.

Still, the young man protested. "It is all wrong," he shouted. "This mountain, the forest, this lake will all be here for ages to come, but I will not."

Perspective. Sometimes we are so wrong. What seems so certain, beyond argument, is actually and totally wrong. On May 18, 1980, volcanic power was unleashed from deep within the mountain and over 1,200 feet of the mountain exploded. The surrounding landscape was instantly destroyed, leveling 3.2 billion feet of timber. Gone was the lake, the cabin, the verdant forest.

Perspective. The higher you are, the better you see. When your head is in heaven, you can see life from a heavenly perspective. You see what really lasts and what really matters. The person who is heavenly minded sets his heart and mind on things above, on the beauty that lasts for all eternity, on love and life for all eternity.

— *L. Keith Whitney*

Reflections

1. "Where your treasure is, there will your heart be also." — Matthew 6:21

2. To be worldly minded is to live for the things of this world. But to be heavenly minded is to live for him who reigns above.

3. We need a new vision of his glory that will restore our sense of Christian purpose and empower us as we serve in his name.

4. "Only with a true vision of heaven burning constantly in our mind's eye can we see with eternal perspective."

5. "One life to live, will soon be past. Only what's done for Christ will last."   — Jim Elliot

6. "Therefore, since we are receiving a kingdom that cannot be shaken, let us be thankful, and so worship God acceptably with reverence and awe."
                                                      — Hebrews 12:28

7. "I went to the root of things, and found nothing but him alone."   — Mira Bai

30

The Garden of God

Somewhere in the distant past, God created this incredible planet we call "Earth." In his own words, everything he made was "good." That seems a remarkable understatement to me. Because I would say that everything he made was fantastic, amazing, beautiful beyond compare!

God himself planted a garden east of Eden, and there he placed the pinnacle of his creative work, the man and the woman. The garden home was quite literally a Paradise, an idyllic existence that predated the coming of weeds, thorns, predators, toxins and ugliness of any kind.

What was this Eden Paradise like? It is not very difficult for me to imagine it. Because I have seen the Swiss Alps, and Yosemite National Park, and Borchard Gardens in Victoria, B.C. I have driven by miles of Iowa cornfields and walked through Southern California orange groves. In Wenatchee, Washington, my family and I breathed the sweet air of orchards filled with pear blossoms. We picked ripe cherries from trees heavy with the luscious red fruit. Yes, I can visualize that primordial Paradise, perfectly prepared for the children of God's love.

For me, one of the experiences of growing older has been the deepening of my appreciation for nature. Probably like you, in my younger years I romped and ran through dazzling beauty and hardly noticed it. Action was the thing. Play hard, have fun! But as I have lived beyond the half-century mark, my sensitivities have been honed. I now marvel at the tiniest living thing I crushed under foot as a child.

But all these reactions to the beauty and wonder of nature are not unique to me. Most people share my appreciation for "Mother Earth." Indeed, some people love nature so dearly that they retreat from the frenetic life of the city into the wilderness. Others just never bother to leave the farm, the ranch, the lake or mountain cabin. Still others involve themselves in the preservation of our natural resources, while activists combat the violence many of us commit against our environment.

Very few of us can stroll through a flower garden without nearly being overcome by the delicate beauty and intoxicating perfume of the colorful array. One of the most impressive features of the creation around us is the endless variety of God's handiwork: flowers of yellow, crimson, lavender, purple, white and nearly every other hue under heaven.

Actually, the more we consider it, the more we realize that *variety* is a central characteristic of creation. Infinite variety. Glorious diversity. And the variations dazzle us when we pause to notice. The wonderful variety of God's creation can be seen in trees and plants, in birds and fish and water mammals, and in amphibians and land animals of all sizes and kinds.

One day as I pondered the marvel of God's diverse world, it dawned on me . . . God has crafted the same wonderful variety into people. He has made dark people and light people and people of shades in between. He has created complexions that are olive and bronze, pink and blue-black. He devised straight hair and curly, almond eyes and round ones, narrow lips and full ones, on and on the variety streams.

Somehow though, the wonder of God's diverse creation is appreciated in nearly every realm except the human one. While we love a bouquet of different, colorful flowers, some of us seem predisposed to like only one or two kinds of people. And while we are fascinated by the various breeds of dogs and cats and horses, some of us are still uncomfortable with the idea of many kinds of people.

But of all the wonders of God's diverse world, the loveliest and most amazing is his triumph of creation: people. Billions of people. Every one different, every one a masterpiece, yet each one handsome in his or her own way. Each person owning a unique and living soul, a Godlike spirit.

May God help us to love, to enjoy, to genuinely *appreciate* the variety and loveliness of His *prize garden* — men and women, girls and boys everywhere. We know we have spiritually matured when we can look into every face — EVERY FACE! — and say, "This, above all, is a lovely flower from the garden of God."

— *Bill Henegar*

Reflections

1. "Jesus loves the little children,
   All the children of the world.
   Red and yellow, black and white,
   They are precious in His sight,
   Jesus loves the little children of the world."
   —Traditional children's song

2. "Beauty is eternity gazing at itself in a mirror."
   — Kahlil Gibran

3. "Somehow though, the wonder of God's diverse creation is appreciated in nearly every realm except the human one."

4. "The real sin against life is to abuse and destroy beauty, even one's own — even more, one's own, for that has been put in our care and we are responsible for its well-being."   — Katherine Anne Porter

5. "To me, fair friend, you never can be old
    For as you were when first your eye I eyed,
    Such seems your beauty still."
                                        — William Shakespeare

6. "We know we have spiritually matured when we can look into every face — EVERY FACE! — and say, 'This, above all, is a lovely flower from the garden of God.'"

7. "I have a dream that one day on the red hills of Georgia the sons of former slaves and the sons of former slaveowners will be able to sit down together at the table of brotherhood."— Martin Luther King, Jr.

31

Loveliness In, Loveliness Out

$\mathcal{W}$e are told in Philippians 4:8 that "whatever is lovely" is among the things that are "excellent or praiseworthy" and that we are to "think on these things." Paul is telling us that "thinking on these things" will make us more wholesome persons. However, this is just the opposite of the way the world thinks.

Not long ago, I met a person who is apparently dying from massive cancer throughout the body. Yet the person's conversation is strongly punctuated with offensive language. This person is frequently seen drinking heavily and is a chain smoker. A friend remarked that this person just will not give up, but is going to live life to the fullest as long as life lasts.

Is **that** really living life to the fullest? Actually, it is directly opposite to what Paul is teaching. For that person, it is not loveliness going in nor is it loveliness coming out. Don't misunderstand me. This person is heavily involved in some meaningful works for humanity. But all of that does not erase the unlovely "other side" of life.

While chiding the crowds for their vain religion, Jesus said: "Listen and understand. What goes into a man's mouth does not make him 'unclean,' but what comes out of his mouth, that is what makes him 'unclean'" (Matthew 15:11). Jesus was responding to the Pharisees who were binding legalities on the people. Jesus responded that the heart of humanity is what must be stressed. Our hearts can be defiled if they are not protected from Satan's defilement.

Jeremiah informs us that "the heart is deceitful above all things and beyond cure. Who can understand it?" (Jeremiah 17:11). Paul wrote, "There is no one righteous, not even one; there is no one who understands, no one who seeks God. All have turned away, they have together become worthless; there is no one who does good, not even one" (Romans 3:10-12). Of course, we all know that Paul was describing the one not redeemed by the blood of Christ and guided by his Spirit. How, then, can we become lovely if our hearts are so wicked?

We can fill our minds with lovely thoughts. Solomon impresses upon us the importance of our hearts (or minds) when he said, "Above all else, guard your heart, for it is the wellspring of life" (Proverbs 4:23). This is a strong expression of the importance of our hearts: "the wellspring of life." Jesus told us that we must control our hearts, "for out of the heart come evil thoughts, murder, adultery, sexual immorality, theft, false testimony, slander. These are what make a man 'unclean'; but eating with unwashed hands does not make him 'unclean'" (Matthew 15:19, 20). If we fill our hearts with lovely thoughts, there will be no room for us to allow evil to come in.

We can associate with the right type of companions. Some time ago, I was asked to play golf with a friend. He brought with him two other men whose language was offensive and whose attitudes toward women were gross. It was miserable to be with them. After two experiences, I told my friend I would be glad to play with him, for he was not offensive. But I did not want to play with the other two men anymore. I did not want my mind filled with the filth that they were releasing from their mouths. Paul told the Corinthians, "Bad company corrupts good character" (1 Corinthians 15:33). Leonardo da Vinci is quoted as saying, "While you are alone you are entirely your own master and if you have one companion you are but half your own." We have to be on guard against how our friends and associates influence us. Keep the kind of company you would not be embarrassed for Jesus to find you with.

We can let our mouths speak things that are lovely. Jesus said: "Out of the overflow of the heart the mouth speaks. The good man brings good things out of the good stored up in him, and the evil man brings evil things out of the evil stored up in him. But I tell you that men will have to give account on the day of judgment for every careless word they have spoken. For by your words you will be acquitted, and by your words you will be condemned" (Matthew 12:34-37). Our words should be concerned with lovely things. If our hearts are thinking lovely things, our mouths will speak them.

There is an expression among computer users that says "garbage in, garbage out" (GIGO). If you put garbage into your computer, you will get garbage out, and often the output will be greatly multiplied. The same is true in our lives: If we put filth and garbage into our hearts, the result will be an outflow of garbage and filth. Let us be sure that we put loveliness in so that we can bring loveliness out.

— *Morris M. Womack*

Reflections

1. How is it possible, or what does it mean, for the heart to be "the wellspring of life"? (see Proverbs 4:23)

2. Consider Leonardo da Vinci's statement, "while you are alone you are entirely your own master and if you have one companion you are but half your own."

3. "By your words you will be acquitted, and by your words you will be condemned." — Matthew 12:37

4. "Create in me a pure heart, O God, and renew a steadfast spirit within me."   — Psalm 51:10

5. "The heart is deceitful above all things and beyond cure. Who can understand it?"   — Jeremiah 17:9

6. "Jesus directly attacked this whole way of thinking [rule-following] when He taught that 'what goes into a man's mouth' (externals) cannot make him unclean. What really disqualifies a person for worship are those things which 'come out of the heart.'"
                                        — Lawrence O. Richards

7. "Purer in heart, O God, Help me to be;
   May I devote my life Wholly to Thee;
   Watch Thou my wayward feet,
   Guide me with counsel sweet;
   Purer in heart, Help me to be."— Fannie C. Davison

32

The Most Excellent Way

$\mathcal{B}$y the time the half-century mark was reached, the first disciples of Christ had blazed trails all over the known world. The good news of Jesus had spread like a raging brushfire. The incendiary message was on the lips of thousands of ordinary people, but it was the apostles, the prophets, the teachers and the miracle workers who were the fearless advance guard. History has never seen such a spiritual blitzkrieg. To many, those were the halcyon days of Christianity. And yet . . .

Something even better was stirring. What could be better than electrifying apostolic messages or prophetic proclamations? What could be more excellent than edifying instruction or astounding miracles? What could be more important than the power to heal or to speak in an unknown tongue?

After discussing marvelous gifts from the Spirit of God such as those, the apostle Paul concluded, "And now I will show you the most excellent way" (1 Corinthians 12:31). The *most excellent* way? Yes, and a way that did not involve any of the abilities, talents or gifts for which we often strive in our lives.

It is natural for most of us to desire prominence, to want to be the preacher or teacher who dazzles others with oratory or to be the spiritual person who amazes others with our depth. That is the way of the natural person — the desire to affirm oneself by grabbing power or popularity or possessions.

However, the truly excellent way is not the natural way. The better way, according to Paul, involves neither affirming ourselves nor being affirmed. Instead, it is characterized by affirming others through patience, protection, faithfulness, kindness and more. The *most excellent* way is love.

But that seems so absurd! How could love possibly be better than prestige or position? The answer Paul gave is a brilliant insight into the nature of things from God's perspective. There will come a time, the apostle said, when the prophet will no longer speak for God. There will be a day when there is no need for unknown tongues or any other miracle. The time is coming when it will no longer be important to teach people about God because every believer will stand in the dazzling presence of the Almighty.

The excellent thing is love. The *eternal* thing is love. Why? Because affirming one another will never be superfluous, but will forever be appropriate. You say, "That may be true someday in heaven, but here, we need prophets, teachers, workers of wonders." Yes, but we need love even more.

The next time you are in a crowd, take a moment to examine the faces of the people you see. Look at each one very carefully and ask, "Does this person need more love?" Rarely, if ever, will the answer be "No." Because every one of us needs to be acknowledged as an individual of worth, as a person who is highly valued. Every one of us needs more love.

If the truth were known, nearly every person has serious doubts concerning his or her importance as an individual. We all know that the world will continue on without us one day — with hardly a blip of notice. Eventually, even the memory of our existence will fade and disappear. However, when love is demonstrated to us, to any one of us, it is like saying: "Your personhood is unique and precious. You will never be forgotten by the God who made you. And you are honored now, in this life!"

If love is the most excellent way, as Paul claimed, then perhaps we take the highest road when our love is the most extraordinary. Perhaps excellence shines its brightest when love is directed at the least likely and most unlovely. And isn't that why people such as Mother Teresa of Calcutta amaze us and bother us so deeply? They are able to love in ways and in places that are uncomfortable, even revolting, to us.

The great days of Christianity were not necessarily those eventful first-century days. Anytime love is the rule in a community, in a church, in a family, in any relationship, the days are bright! That is because love is the most profound miracle of all. God can shake open a prison and loosen the chains of his followers. He can heal a sick person. He can raise the dead. But he cannot, or will not, change our hearts against our will. However, when we open ourselves to love, the greatest of all miracles occurs. We care for one another. And the world is renewed and revolutionized.

No love on earth can approach the sublime excellence of the love God demonstrated in Christ Jesus. When we were at our lowest, our dirtiest, our most unlovely, Christ died for the ungodly. That selfless sacrifice became the paradigm for love, the perfect example of the most excellent way. Better than prophecy, better than miracles, better even than biblical knowledge . . . is love. And it takes no special power, no special talent, no special understanding. Just love. In the Spirit of the loving Savior.

— *Bill Henegar*

Reflections

1. "My command is this: Love each other as I have loved you." — John 15:12

2. "The excellent thing is love. The *eternal* thing is love. Why? Because affirming one another will never be superfluous."

3. "I love you with the love of the Lord.
   I love you with the love of the Lord;
   I see in you the glory of my King,
   And I love you with the love of the Lord."
   — Jim Gilbert

4. "Love is the only sane and satisfactory answer to the problem of human existence."   — Erich Fromm

5. "Perhaps excellence shines its brightest when love is directed at the least likely and most unlovely."

6. "Love cures people, the ones who receive love and the ones who give it, too."   — Karl A. Menninger

7. "Dear friends, let us love one another, for love comes from God. Everyone who loves has been born of God and knows God."   — 1 John 4:7

33

Celebrate Love

*I*n *Acts of Love*, Alice Gray tells a nice little story about a mother who came home after a long, hard day of work. Her little daughter ran out of the house to greet her. "Mommy, mommy, wait until I tell you what happened today." After listening to a few words, the mother responded by indicating the rest could wait as she needed to get dinner ready. But during the meal, the phone rang, other family members' stories were longer and louder, and other seemingly more urgent concerns cluttered the evening. After the kitchen was cleaned and brother's homework questions were answered, the little girl tried once again to get her mother's attention. But by then it was time for her to get ready for bed.

Mother came to tuck her little girl into bed and listen to her prayers. As she bent down to tousle the little girl's curls and lovingly kiss her soft cheek, the child looked up and asked, "Mommy, do you really love me even if you don't have time to listen to me?"

Wow! When I read those words, my mind raced across the years of law practice, ministry, teaching, my sports activities and other distractions. How many times did work, television or some other equally "urgent activity" keep me from just listening to my little girls? How many times did I fail to have time for my wife?

I confess to you that I was able to remember more

instances of selfish inattention than of times of caring attention. I can think of far too few times when I have interrupted the routine busy-ness of life to love my life's most precious gifts. I wish I could tell you that I lived with a sense of celebrating the love I have for my wife and daughters. But I didn't have time.

The structure of this book is organized around "thinking about" the lovely, the pure and the virtuous, but just beyond the "thinking about" text in Philippians is another crucial text: "Whatever you have learned or received or heard from me, or seen in me — *put into practice*" (Philippians 4:9).

Into practice. Some may celebrate love with beautifully poetic words. Others celebrate with flowers, romantic trips and lavish gifts. However, the most lavish way to simply celebrate love is to take the time to listen to the one you love. I am talking about turning the television off, ending other distractive noise and really listening to the other you love. Such action will say to the other that at that moment he or she is more important than anything else in your life.

Perhaps noise is best ended and love best celebrated by taking time to get away from it all. Celebrating love requires commitment and discipline. You may need to schedule time for your loved ones. Make a date with your mate! Ask your child to go out with you by giving him or her an invitation to a "Just-You-and-Me Day." In all this activity, remember to keep the other in your heart and mind and to just listen.

I have not done nearly as much of this as I would like to tell you I have. But the few moments when we have been away from television, deadlines, telephones and other noise have been the most rewarding for us. I have been blessed through the privilege of teaching at one of the great universities of America. Pepperdine University has one of the best international programs of any of America's universities. We were chosen to participate as the host family at our Heidelberg, Germany, campus. It was thrilling to visit numerous countries and historical cities, but the truly wonderful blessing was the time apart from normal distractions. We walked the quaint streets, sipped coffee in intimate shops, and just talked and talked. Each of us cherishes the time together more than the memories of places visited.

My message to myself, as well as my point for all to ponder, is that we cannot afford to wait for teaching terms in Heidelberg. Most of us will never have such an opportunity. But, as we live each day of our lives, we have the opportunity to take the time to celebrate love and another life. All we have to do is turn off the television, turn the answering machine on, and make a commitment to listen. Do it! God will bless you richly. I promise.

— *L. Keith Whitney*

Reflections

1. Do you really love someone if you have no time to listen to him or to her?

2. "Perhaps noise is best ended and love best celebrated by taking time to get away from it all."

3. "Mankind owes to the child the best it has to give."
   — Opening words of the United Nations'
   Declaration of the Rights of the Child

4. "The most important thing a father can do for his children is to love their mother."
   — Theodore M. Hesburgh

5. "To every thing there is a season, and a time to every purpose under the heaven."   — Ecclesiates 3:1 KJV

6. Take time for your children. "... bring them up in the training and instruction of the Lord" (Ephesians 6:4).

7. "Time is every man's angel."   — A saying

Things That Are
ADMIRABLE

34

Let's Face It

*H*is office door was always open. And it accommodated a nearly constant stream of people — some needing his sage advice, others needing assurance of their personal worth and still others wanting nothing more than a word of cheer. For the latter, he was prepared with a joke or a cartoon, which he shared along with his hardy, infectious machine-gun-like laugh. For the former, he had a Bible nearby. And a prayer. And a message of encouragement.

It was no accident that people sought him out when they were perplexed or dejected. He tempted everyone into his love with jars of candy, a bubble gum machine, a drawer full of chips and peanuts and a small refrigerator stocked with a variety of soft drinks. Every passerby knew he or she was welcome to anything in the tiny office, with its packed bookshelves reaching to the ceiling.

Ah, but it was not just the availability of the goodies that made you feel welcome there. It was his broad smile, his soft eyes, his ready laugh and his equally ready tears.

Everyone called him "Big" Don. Yes, he was six-foot-five and a shade more than 200 pounds — okay, 240. But we all knew that the "Big" in Big Don really referred to the size of his heart. It was so big that nobody was excluded.

The Bible has a fair amount to say about hospitality. And once in a while, we even talk a little about it in our churches. Nearly all of the time, though, we speak of hospitality as the act of welcoming people into our homes. But there is something much more important than opening our front doors to people. And that is opening our lives to them. And even *opening our faces.*

Opening our faces? How do we do that? We do it the way Big Don Williams did it: We smile when we approach someone; we relax our gaze and let our eyes say, "You are safe with me"; we speak warmly and without condemnation; and we send out an attitude signal that communicates to each person that he or she is of great value and significance.

Jesus had that kind of face. Was his face round or long, dark or pale, chiseled or fleshy? We don't know — and it doesn't really matter. But we do know this, and it does really matter: his was an open, welcoming face. The kind of face that encouraged a long-ill woman to reach out and touch his robe. And a member of the Jewish high council to seek him out for a personal interview. And a Gentile soldier to come and ask for the healing of his daughter. And a hated tax collector to climb a tree for just one glimpse of him. And a ragtag band of fishermen and dropouts to follow him to the ends of the earth.

Show hospitality. Open your doors to the poor and the not-so-poor. But even more important in a closed-face and hostile world, welcome people into your heart. How can they enter your heart? Through your face! Your eyes will say, "Come in." Your expression will say, "I care." Your smile will say, "You have nothing to fear from me. I love you."

Children are often incredibly perceptive. They are able to scan a room, somehow identify the gentlest person and quickly toddle in that direction. How do they do it? At an early age, humans develop a certain sense that recognizes sincerity and kindness in a face. Children can also recognize a stern face or an uninterested face.

As we grow up, we retain that ability to find an open face. In a mall full of shoppers or in a flood of pedestrians along a city sidewalk, we search the oncoming sea of faces for a hint of friendliness. If we find it, it warms us for a moment.

But also as we grow up, we learn to cover our faces — for an open face reveals a soul. And we often don't want people to look inside us. There is too much duplicity within. So we cover our faces with layers of preoccupation, busyness, suspicion, blankness — and we become part of the sea of closed faces.

Before we can welcome people into our heart, we must allow God to cleanse our heart. Day by day, our inner person needs that purging. Then, when God has forgiven us and made us pure, we are able to open our faces to one another without hypocrisy.

Practice hospitality. Open your doors to people, especially people who need God. But even better, *open your face to them.* Like Big Don did. And like Jesus did.

— *Bill Henegar*

Reflections

1. "It is a sin against hospitality to open your doors and shut up your countenance."   — A proverb

2. "Open your doors to the poor and the not-so-poor. But even more important in a closed-faced and hostile world, welcome people into your heart."

3. "You will notice we say brother
   and sister 'round here,
   It's because we're a family
   and these folks are so near.
   When one has a heartache we all share the tears,
   And rejoice in each vict'ry in this family so dear."
   — William J. Gaither

4. "Do not forget to entertain strangers, for by so doing some people have entertained angels without knowing it."   — Hebrews 13:2

5. "Before we can welcome people into our heart, we must allow God to cleanse our heart. Day by day, our inner person needs that purging."

6. "For I was hungry and you gave me something to eat, I was thirsty and you gave me something to drink, I was a stranger and you invited me in, I needed clothes and you clothed me, I was sick and you looked after me, I was in prison and you came to visit me."
                                                       — Matthew 25:35, 36

7. "Love bade me welcome: yet my soul drew back,
   Guilty of dust and sin.
   But quick-eyed Love, observing me grow slack,
   From my first entrance in,
   Drew nearer to me, sweetly questioning,
   If I lacked anything."   — George Herbert

35

Offering Hospitality

$\mathcal{A}$s I sit reminiscing about my life, I think of two very important people in particular. This husband and wife were among the most hospitable people I have ever known. Their home became a "home" for me and my bride of little more than a year. Over the course of nearly three years of our lives, we spent many precious hours with them.

We often went to their home following Sunday morning worship and drank deeply of their Christian hospitality. We truly became honorary members of their family. Visiting with these unusual Christians instilled two permanent values that have contributed to our Christian experience. First, we learned the blessing of offering and receiving hospitality. Second, we learned the values, techniques and rewards of personal evangelism. You see, after we finished eating and the dishes were cleaned, the four of us would spend much of the remainder of the afternoon practicing hospitality by visiting the sick, those absent from worship, and others who had need.

Undoubtedly, these two types of events — different in many ways, and yet so complementary to each other — molded our younger minds and implanted in our hearts some valuable lessons. I learned how to do personal visitation from the husband, who was one of the dedicated

elders of that church. We also learned the values of showing love and hospitality to others. My own life has
probably been shaped by these people more than I can
ever know.

I want to share with you some of the tremendous values of hospitality to the meaningful development of the
Christian spirit. Much is written about hospitality in
Scripture. Perhaps the one verse that leaps into my mind
is, "Do not forget to entertain strangers, for by so doing
some people have entertained angels without knowing
it" (Hebrews 13:2). I once heard a fable about a man who
was told that the Lord would visit him on a certain day.
He hurried to do all the chores of readying the house for
the visit. A hungry beggar came by, but he was told "I
have no time to feed you now. The Lord is coming."
Later, one who was ill and needed care and comfort
asked for help, and he received the same reply. Near the
end of the day, a man came by asking to be taught about
the Lord, and he too was told that he should come later
when the host had time to help. Very late that night, the
Lord appeared to the man who asked the Lord why he
hadn't come. The Lord said: "I came three times today —
first as a beggar, second as a sick person, and third as one
wanting to be taught. You did not receive me any of these
times."

Is our hospitality like this? Do we often not recognize
the opportunity to "entertain strangers"? In the reference
above, many may be referred to; but the one person who
had this experience was undoubtedly Abraham. "The
Lord appeared to Abraham near the great trees of
Mamre. . . . Abraham looked up and saw three men
standing nearby" (Genesis 18:1, 2). These three men were
not *ordinary men*, but probably angels. Yet, Abraham did
not know he was talking to angels. Notice in the preceding verses that Abraham exercised hospitality toward
these "men" sent from God. Paul writes us that elders
(bishops) should be hospitable (1 Timothy 3:2; Titus 1:8);
widows who are "put on the list of widows" should be

"showing hospitality" (1 Timothy 5:10); and all Christians should "practice hospitality" (Romans 12:13).

It would seem that our day is one in which hospitality is not as prominent as in earlier times. We appear too busy, too other-involved, to be able to practice hospitality. The word "hospitality" is closely related to the word "hospital," which is a part of the word. In showing concern for others, we certainly become a sort of "hospice" or "hospital" to those whom we invite into our homes, or when we show hospitality to those who are a part of our Christian family. The same care should be shown to those who visit church services. Churches should be known as hospitable groups of people. Let us never lose the sense of welcome and hospitality no matter how large our churches may become.

— *Morris M. Womack*

Reflections

1. "A guest never forgets the host who had treated him kindly."   — Homer

2. "Then Jesus said to his host, 'When you give a luncheon or dinner, do not invite your friends, your brothers or relatives, or your rich neighbors; if you do, they may invite you back and so you will be repaid.'"
                                                    — Luke 14:12

3. What is involved in the act of hospitality? How can I know I have been a hospitable person?

4. Do we often not recognize the opportunity to "entertain strangers"? (see Hebrews 13:2)

5. What has caused our generation to be so other-
   involved as to neglect hospitality? How can we remedy this?

6. In the light of Genesis 18:1ff., how can Abraham be a
   role model for us in the area of Christian hospitality?

7. Hospitality was a very important part of ancient culture. Why have we lost that virtue in our society, and
   how can we bring it back?

36

Random Kindness and Senseless Acts of Beauty

*I*t has been said that "the world is going to hell in a handbasket." Where are all of the nice people who used to be so kind and courteous? Has chivalry died? Are there now no "random acts of kindness" or "senseless acts of beauty"? Has the world of kindness actually gone "to hell in a handbasket"? I don't think so. Certainly we often see acts of rudeness or crudeness all around us. We hear of many by way of the media telling of those who have no concern for others. We hear of those whose philosophy of life is "what is yours is mine, and I will take it from you." But, there are still many good people who care about others' rights.

Recently, I played golf with a man I had never seen before and whom I probably will never see again. After I got home, I noticed that my appointment book containing my checkbook was missing. Later that evening, I got a call from this man with whom I had played golf, calling to tell me that he had found my appointment book with the checkbook. He wanted to assure me that he had found it and was mailing it to me. There was no worldly reason why he should have done this except the presence of a random act of kindness by a very nice and honest gentleman. Perhaps you can remember a time someone was unusually nice when it really wasn't expected. It was done simply because the person wanted to be nice.

You never know what will happen when you perform some random kindness or senseless act of beauty for someone. The writer of the book of Hebrews reminds us to "keep on loving each other as brothers. Do not forget to entertain strangers, for by so doing some people have entertained angels without knowing it" (Hebrews 13:1, 2).

God is a God of kindness. Abraham's chief servant declared this when he prayed, "O Lord, God of my master Abraham, give me success today, and show kindness to my master Abraham" (Genesis 24:12). David cried out to God, "You are kind and forgiving, O Lord, abounding in love to all who call to you" (Psalm 86:5). And God himself told the Israelites of his kindness. "'Let him who boasts boast about this: That he understands and knows me, that I am the Lord, who exercises kindness, justice and righteousness on earth, for in these I delight, declares the Lord" (Jeremiah 9:24). If we want to be like God, we will exercise kindness and senseless acts of beauty toward our fellow human beings. We need to let our fellowship with God be seen in the nature of our own behavior.

Jesus is the master example of kindness. His life was one of kindness. I think of the Canaanite woman who came to Jesus asking him to heal her daughter. After playing word games with the woman to show her faith, Jesus healed the woman's daughter (Matthew 15:21-28). Or, recall the time Jesus healed the leper (Matthew 8:1-5); or when He bade Peter to walk on the water to show that he could calm the sea and save Peter's life (Matthew 9:23-27).

Jesus' plan for his followers was that they live as kind and loving people. In his extraordinary Sermon on the Mount, Jesus declared, "In everything, do to others what you would have them do to you, for this sums up the Law and the Prophets" (Matthew 7:12). This statement has been called "The Golden Rule." In common parlance, it sounds like this: "Do unto others as you would have them do unto you." What a wonderful world this would be if everyone based their lives on the principles of the Golden Rule.

Does this principle work in real life? When we practice "random kindness and senseless acts of beauty," does this **ever** influence people to change their behavior? It certainly does! Paul has this to say, "Bless those who persecute you. . . . Do not repay anyone evil for evil. Be careful to do what is right in the eyes of everybody. If it is possible, as far as it depends on you, live at peace with everyone. Do not take revenge, my friends. . . . If your enemy is hungry, feed him; if he is thirsty, give him something to drink. In doing this, you will heap burning coals on his head" (Romans 12:14-20). The ideal life of God's person is to live a selfless life.

The key word describing the selfless life is love (*agape*). *Agape* describes an unusual level of love. It exclaims, "You cannot stop me from loving you. You may mistreat me; you may reject me, but I will love you anyway!" *Agape* is a word which suggests that we will exercise a selfless good will and a wish for good for everyone. This is a difficult challenge; but *it will work*. Try it!

— Morris M. Womack

Reflections

1. Think of times when you have witnessed and/or performed "random acts of kindness" when there was no earthly reason why you should have done them. If you did them, how did you feel after having done them?

2. "In everything, do to others what you would have them do to you, for this sums up the Law and the Prophets."   — Matthew 7:12

3. What is the meaning of Paul's statement when he says, "If your enemy is hungry, feed him; if he is thirsty, give him something to drink. In doing this,

you will heap burning coals on his head"? (see Romans 12:14-20)

4. Think about this idea: "There is a courtesy of the heart. It is akin to love. Out of it arises the purest courtesy in the outward behavior."   — Goethe

5. In what way(s) do you think your practicing the *agape* sort of love would change your life for the better?

6. Does the fact that God's church is divided into local, congregational units suggest that God wants us to exercise "fellowship" and personal communion with one another?

7. "I expect to pass through life but once. If therefore, there be any kindness I can show, or any good thing I can do to any fellow being, let me do it now, and not defer or neglect it, as I shall not pass this way again."
                                        — William Penn

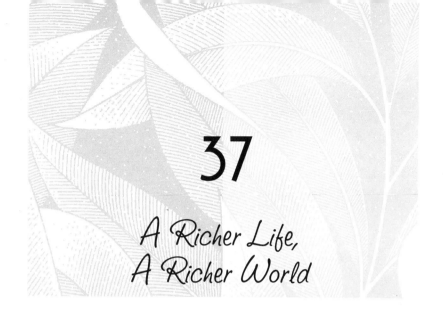

37

A Richer Life, A Richer World

One day Jesus was traveling along the border between Samaria and Galilee on his way to Jerusalem. Apparently, his reputation had preceded him because as he approached a certain village, ten men with leprosy came toward him. They halted some distance from him and shouted, "Jesus, Master, have pity on us!"

Jesus simply said, "Go, show yourselves to the priests." Miraculously, they were healed as they hurried toward the local holy men. Their willingness to obey Jesus' command indicated their faith in him as Master and in his ability to heal them.

But one of the ten lepers had more than faith. When he looked down and saw his cleansed body, he turned around in amazement and ran back toward Jesus, shouting praises to God. He fell down at the feet of Jesus and thanked him for a new chance at life. The man was a Samaritan. And Jesus said, "Were not all ten cleansed? Where are the other nine? Was no one found to return and give praise to God except this foreigner?" Then he said to the Samaritan, "Rise and go; your faith has made you well."

Only one out of ten. Perhaps that is the approximate number of thankful people in an average group at any given time. Or perhaps it is the proportion of time you and I typically remember to thank and praise our God.

Certainly, thankfulness is as rare a commodity today as it was two millennia ago.

But so what? What difference does it make anyway? Yes, it is polite and nice to be thankful, but it is difficult to remember to be nice in a crowded, busy world like ours. However, being thankful is much more than just being polite. Remembering to give thanks is one way God changes our life and our outlook.

The wonderful, soaring Psalm 100 instructs us to "enter his gates with thanksgiving and his courts with praise; give thanks to him and praise his name." This is not only a command, it is good advice for those who want to have a positive view of life and good mental health. "ENTER with thanksgiving and praise," the psalmist said. It is the activity with which we *approach* God. And we will do well to approach our daily lives the same way.

Jesus himself followed the prescription. In the model prayer he shared with his disciples, he began, "Our Father in heaven, hallowed be your name, your kingdom come, your will be done on earth as it is in heaven." This is lofty praise that acknowledges the place of God in the scheme of things.

The more we remember to thank God, the more we realize our blessedness. That is important because we often tend to focus only on the things we *do not* have. When we acknowledge that every leaf on every tree, every creature that has life, every breath we take *and every lovely thing* is a gift to us from God, we minimize our "needs" and "wants."

Even more, when we praise God for his power, his steadfastness, his goodness, his love and his nearness, we acknowledge the source of strength that can replace our weaknesses. Praising God reminds us that he is able to heal all our wounds and take away all our sins and cares. When we proclaim his sufficiency, we dispel our "poor me" complex and tap into the true source of power.

Thanking and praising God are activities that benefit

us rather than him. He does not need our thanksgiving and praise, but we need the perspective those activities give us.

There is another important aspect to this business of thankfulness. When we remember to thank another person for a kindness directed toward us, we remind ourselves of how God works through people. It makes us aware of the pinpoints of light in this dark world. And our thanks warms the heart of the giver of kindness and encourages him or her to continue acts of kindness.

Likewise, when we praise another person, we reinforce that person's self-esteem and promote positive traits. No one will ever know what greatness has been wrought in the lives of people by a little praise at just the right moment.

A surprising thing about thanksgiving and praise is that they cost us nothing — they are only words — yet they accomplish amazing things. Another surprising thing, as Jesus knew, is that the world is poorer because of the scarcity of those simple words. Interesting isn't it? They cost us nothing, but they make us richer by far.

— *Bill Henegar*

Reflections

1. "Enter his gates with thanksgiving and his courts with praise; give thanks to him and praise his name."
    — Psalm 100

2. "Remembering to give thanks is one way God changes our life and our outlook."

3. "Then a voice came from the throne, saying: 'Praise our God, all you his servants, you who fear him, both small and great!' Then I heard what sounded like a great multitude, like the roar of rushing waters and

like loud peals of thunder, shouting: 'Hallelujah! For our Lord God Almighty reigns. Let us rejoice and be glad and give him glory!'"   — Revelation 19:5-7

4. "The more we remember to thank God, the more we realize our blessedness."

5. "Be joyful always; pray continually; give thanks in all circumstances, for this is God's will for you in Christ Jesus."   — 1 Thessalonians 5:16-18

6. "Thanking and praising God is an activity that benefits us rather than him."

7. "Lord, for the erring thought
    Not into evil wrought:
    Lord, for the wicked will
    Betrayed and baffled still:
    For the heart from itself kept,
    Our thanksgiving accept." — William Dean Howells

38

Friends

*T*here are three kinds of friends in this life. The first kind is what I would call "fair-weather friends." Proverbs 18:24 says, "A man of many friends comes to ruin . . . ." In other words, we can surround ourselves with lots of "friends" who will stand with us as long as there's something in it for them. But when the storms come, they're gone. When we are no longer valuable to them or when we become a liability in some way, they drop us like a bad habit.

The last part of Proverbs 18:24 speaks of the second kind of friend. The passage continues, ". . . but there is a friend who sticks closer than a brother." That is the person who is "true-blue," who will be there for you in the worst of times as well as the best. Popularity or power or money can't buy friends like that. Even if you haven't nurtured the friendship as you should (and you should!), that kind of friend will immediately overlook your mistakes or your neglect and rush to your aid when you are in distress. That kind of friend is hard to find. So when you discover such a person, be a friend in return and value him or her highly.

Perhaps the best definition of this second kind of friend is found in Proverbs 17:17. There it says, "A friend loves at all times, and a brother is born for adversity." That is it, isn't it? We know many people who are supportive *some of* the time, but a true friend is one who loves *at all times*. Even when we don't deserve to be loved. Such a friend is just like a blood-brother who stands with you in adversity, who fights beside you to the very end, who seems to be born for such a time.

Then there is a third kind of friend, one that is just like the one mentioned above, with one additional characteristic: He or she is a true *Christian* friend. Singer and songwriter Michael W. Smith says it well: "And friends are friends forever, if the Lord's the Lord of them; and a friend will not say never, 'cause the welcome will not end. Though it's hard to let you go, in the Father's hands we know that a lifetime's not too long to live as friends." Michael is right. There are some friends who will be our friends to the very end. However, there are other friends who will be our friends *beyond the end* . . . to the beginning of forever! They are *Christians*, and they will inherit eternal life with us. And they are the best kind of friends of all.

Who doesn't want to have friends like that? But we should remember, as Christians, that we are called, not to *have* a friend, but to *be a friend.* Jesus gave us brilliant insight into what that means. In John 15:13, he said, "No one has greater love than the one who lays down his life for his friends." That is the supreme moment and the acid test of friendship: Will we die for a friend? And of course, that is exactly what Jesus did for each of us.

Jesus continued in the passage to talk about our response to his friendship. He said, "You are my friends if you do what I command." We sometimes talk of God's grace supplanting the "old law." But we would do well to remember that friendship with Jesus is contingent upon obedience — not perfect obedience, to be sure, but obedience to his commands, nonetheless. As his friends, we have been brought into both his confidence and his mission. He continued, "I no longer call you servants, because a servant does not know his master's business. Instead, I have called you friends, for everything that I learned from my Father I have made known to you." Yes, we serve the Lord and one another as *servants*. But Jesus has graced us by lifting us above the level of uninformed, unmotivated servants by calling us *friends* and *brothers* and *sisters*. How great is his love for us! And how great is our debt to him.

Think about friendship. Better yet, think about your very best friend. And now think about the supreme Friend of humanity, Jesus Christ. No one has greater love than the one who lays down his life for his friends. Jesus said that. And Jesus did that. What a friend we have in Jesus! What a friend he calls us to be.

— *Bill Henegar*

Reflections

1. "A man of many companions may come to ruin, but there is a friend who sticks closer than a brother."
— Proverbs 18:24

2. "Without friendship and the openness and trust that go with it, skills are barren and knowledge may become an unguided missile."
— Frank H.T. Rhodes

3. "A friend loves at all times, and a brother is born for adversity." — Proverbs 17:17

4. "So long as we are loved by others I should say that we are almost indispensable; and no man is useless while he has a friend." — Robert Louis Stevenson

5. "No one has greater love than the one who lays down his life for his friends. You are my friends if you do what I command. I no longer call you servants, because a servant does not know his master's busi-

ness. Instead, I have called you friends, for everything
that I learned from my Father I have made known to
you."   — John 15:13-15

6. "What a Friend we have in Jesus,
    All our sins and griefs to bear;
    What a privilege to carry
    Ev'rything to God in prayer.
    O what peace we often forfeit,
    O what needless pain we bear,
    All because we do not carry
    Ev'rything to God in prayer."
                                    — Joseph M. Scriven

7. "A true friend is the best possession."
                                    — Benjamin Franklin

39

The Ministry of Blessing

"The right word spoken at the right time is as beautiful as gold apples in a silver bowl." — *Proverbs 25:11*

I am convinced that people really do *need* other people. We were simply not made to live alone. *Without love and the touch of those who love us, we wither and die.* Oh, maybe we don't physically die, at least not all at once, but we certainly die in spirit. Something inside us, something vital, just withers and dies.

We all need to feel special to others we love or who love us. People who feel rejected by others begin to feel like a nobody. Feeling the self-doubt, isolation or loneliness of rejection, some people rudely push others away in anticipation of their own rejection. Others get caught up in self-verification by constantly trying to prove to themselves that they are not a nobody.

What do we do? Well, many people try to prove that they are somebody by their physical appearance or sexual attractiveness or prowess. Others base their self-image on their possessions and acquisitions. Finally, our desires for social status, power and prestige are often just a defense against feelings of inferiority. However, we usually discover such false pursuits ultimately fail. Inside we still feel fear and insecurity; we are filled with self-doubt and loneliness.

What do we really need? Again I say: **What we really**

need is to feel special to others we love or who love us. We
need to be blessed.

In the Bible, "blessing" means many things. One concept conveyed by the word is the transfer of favor.
"Blessing" may be conferred by words spoken or by
action. But blessing always involves the one giving the
blessing, recognizing and conveying the positive attributes of the one being blessed. **Blessing affirms.** It recognizes the gifts and abilities of the one receiving the
blessing.

Deep inside we die a little when we hear that little echo
of a voice continually repeating: "You can't do it. You can't
do anything right. You're dumb." Or perhaps: "You are
about the worst singer I ever heard. Oh, and you're ugly
too!" I still remember cutting words spoken to me as a
child. Some accurately described the first efforts of an
overweight child trying to play baseball or basketball. But
no matter how good I became, no matter how many
awards I won, I could not erase that monotonous voice
inside. It kept telling me I could not play well.

At a conference of college teachers who were inter-
ested in improving their teaching, the facilitator asked us
to list the best teacher with whom we had been privi-
leged to study. The conference was a number of years
ago, and I have often thought about my answer. The man
I named was brilliant and articulate. But I named him
because he had impressed me with *his* brilliance. In fact,
he had done nothing to help me find my way in the
world. Now, after all these years, I would answer the
question differently. I believe he failed as a teacher.

Doesn't that observation apply to the preachers, the
parents, the managers and other leaders of this world? Is
the truly great preacher the one who impresses us the
most with his oratorical style or his wit? Is it possible that
the truly gifted teacher is the person Jesus describes as
the one who humbles herself and serves others? *The most
important teacher you will ever have is the teacher who
blesses you*, the teacher who helps you to see your gifts

and talents and assists you in forming a vision of a ful-filling future, using your gifts to touch and help others.

How can you be a blessing to others? How can you be a parent who blesses your children? I believe there are many, many ways to bless others, but I also see some helpful clues in the text of God's Word.

For example, have you ever noticed how the names of biblical figures almost always have important meanings? The name of Barnabas conveys "encouragement," and he lived encouraging others. An apostle once nicknamed "son of thunder" was later affirmed as an "apostle of love." So nicknamed, he wrote more about the love of God than any other writer. He is the writer who told us that the mark of a disciple of Jesus is love for others.

One very practical suggestion I have for you, if you are a parent, is to **give your child positive nicknames**. Recognize your son's or daughter's gifts by attaching affirming phrases to his or her name. Let your child hear you tell others about his or her special gifts. Write positives on their hearts.

Affirm your child's positive qualities in other creative ways. Buy a pack of chewing gum or a piece of your child's favorite candy, and slip a note inside the outer wrapper of each piece. In each note, list one of the qualities about your child that you most admire. "I am amazed at the kind and caring way you care for other children." "You write so well. I believe you could be an author of books some day."

Even if you are not a gifted poet, you might **try writing a brief funny poem** (the crazier the better) **to your child**. Affirm your daughter or son in your poem, and affirm your love for her or him. Tell your son or daughter, "I will never give up on you."

I hope you see that the ideas are limitless. Every time you have a chance to catch your child doing something good, clap and cheer, and say, "Great job!" Maintain an encouraging, positive attitude toward each child's art work, first attempts to write and first efforts at sports.

One of the greatest coaches I have ever known was a high school coach in the small town in which I grew up. He later coached college ball. But I was a gym rat, so I hung around him all the time. I was always at the baseball diamond or on a basketball floor. Now, you have to understand that at the time I knew him I was probably fifteen pounds overweight and slow. I was living evidence of the movie title, "White Men Can't Jump!" I did a lot of things wrong and not many things right. But he noticed one of the few things I did well. I had good court vision and could pass the basketball well. He encouraged what I did well. He helped me envision becoming a great "assists" man.

Years later, I realized that that was what he did for everyone. He saw what each player could do to help a team win, and he affirmed and developed those gifts. His teams still hold the highest winning percentages in the history of my hometown. He helped others contribute by being the best they could be at what they did well and, in the process, made winners out of everyone.

Do you want children who have a healthy sense of self-esteem? Do you want to be a part of a "winning" family, church, office or any other team? Then learn to bless others by affirming their gifts and helping them to envision a bright future. Help others see how they can make a positive contribution by using their gifts to the glory of God. Be a blesser! Everyone, including yourself, will be blessed.

— *L. Keith Whitney*

Reflections

1. We need to feel special to others we love or who love us. We need to be blessed.

2. Without love and the touch of those who love us, we wither and die.

3. Tell your son or daughter, "I will never give up on you."

4. God said to Abraham, "All peoples on earth will be blessed through you" (Genesis 12:3).

5. Encouragement is affirming others and the work they are doing for God. "The right word spoken at the right time is as beautiful as gold apples in a silver bowl" (Proverbs 25:11).

6. To bless someone in biblical times meant many things. It meant to praise them, to pray for them and to commit them to God's care. It also meant to dedicate and challenge them to live forever committed to God.

7. Jeremiah 17:7 in NLB, ". . . blessed are those who trust in the LORD and have made the LORD their hope and confidence." Thus, blessings are not just words spoken by a parent, but a special relationship offered by God.

Things That Are
EXCELLENT

40

Fulfilling Our Potential

$\mathcal{C}$harles Dudley Warner said it well, "What small potatoes we all are, compared with what we might be!" So many of us allow life's circumstances or the narrow vision of others to define who we can be or what we can accomplish. But I believe that true genius lies in envisioning life or success or something else no one else can see, setting about to make it happen, and achieving beyond the limitations that most would place on us. If you can envision a brighter tomorrow, you can achieve it!

The problem is that we can get distracted so easily from our dreams. Defeat or failure can cause us to doubt or give up. Listening to the reality therapy so-called friends will apply to our problems can also cause discouragement. "You are too ambitious!" "You expect too much!" "You are a dreamer. Get real!" "Just get a job and make some money. People from our background cannot make a difference." We settle for the routine. We become what others expect us to become. We live life according to the dictates and expectations of others.

Perhaps you saw the Bette Midler movie *Beaches*. As I remember the story, it involved two girls who met on Atlantic City's Boardwalk. One, Bette's character, was a vaudevillian performer who pursued her dreams with relentless energy, forever envisioning her debut in Hollywood. The other girl was wealthy and sophisticated.

While Bette followed her dreams and her heart, the other lived according to the expectations of her family. Even her college major resulted from her perception of the family's expectations.

In the end, the woman from a background of wealth and privilege was divorced and dying. She had been educated in the best universities. She lived in a beautiful house surrounded by all the outward trappings of success. But following her death, she wanted Bette's character to raise her daughter. Why?

I believe she wanted her daughter to learn to risk disapproval, even failure, as she pursued her dreams. She wanted her child to become all God intended her to be, or at least to learn the joy of knowing what it means to die having given life all you have. Robert Browning gives us a glimpse of the same truth in his memorable quote about vision: "A man's reach should exceed his grasp, or what's a heaven for?" Big dreaming makes people bigger. We edge toward fulfilling the potential with which God created us.

Although the movie *Beaches* was a masterful blend of triumph and tragedy, I cried long before we learned that the young mother was dying. My tears flowed from the pain of knowing that I had given up on my dreams. I had followed my heart in leaving the beauty of Pepperdine University to preach for a church in California. In my view, I had failed, and we decided to move back to the Midwest. As I sat watching the movie, I was alone and hurting with the gray days of the Illinois winter reflecting my soul's depression. I had given up. We had returned to Illinois to be closer to family, to lick our wounds and to settle for a more realistic life.

Since those gray, overcast days, I have learned some important lessons. I now understand that we serve an extraordinary God, who continually uses ordinary people of faith to do amazing things. Dreams flow from our God-given potential; they result from who he created us to be. If you repeatedly see a brighter tomorrow, you *can* achieve it! If you can get involved, you can make things happen. If you can only begin, you can continue; if you can climb, you can climb even higher. You can go as far as your dreams and your faith can take you.

Reportedly, William Borden, heir to the Borden Dairy estate, chose to become a missionary to China. He wrote in his Bible, "No reservations." He entered seminary and worked hard toward his goal. Rejecting the temptation to give up his dream and accept the role of privilege and power ever available to him, he wrote, "No retreats." Later, before his death in Egypt on his journey to China, he wrote, "No regrets."

Isn't that what fulfilling our potential is all about? When we peel off the cocoon wrappings of fear, defeat and discouragement and discover our wings, we know the joy of flight. Jesus took a bunch of cowering, defeated fishermen, tax collectors, and sinners, breathed his Spirit into them and freed them to fly. In a few short years, these insignificant peasants from "Zip Code 00000" turned the world upside down. Will you allow him to empower you to fulfill your potential? Will you let his Spirit give you the power to use your wings and fly? Just believe!

— *L. Keith Whitney*

Reflections

1. "A man's reach should exceed his grasp, or what's a heaven for?"   — Robert Browning

2. "What small potatoes we all are, compared with what we might be!"   — Charles Dudley Warner

3. "We are what our thoughts have made us; so take care about what you think. Words are secondary. Thoughts live; they travel far."   — Vivekananda

4. "Genius . . . means little more than the faculty of perceiving in an inhabitual way."   — William James

5. "Commit your work to the Lord, and then your plans will succeed."   — Proverbs 16:3 NLT

6. "Be honest in your estimate of yourselves, measuring your value by how much faith God has given you."
                                    — Romans 12:3 NLT

7. You can go as far as your dreams and your faith can take you.

41

The Designs of God

Excellence is a difficult concept to define. It is both the winning effort of the champion and the losing effort of the person who tried with all of his or her heart. Excellence can be thought of as the best, the highest, the finest. Or it can be understood as achieving one's potential. Perhaps for the Christian, the most meaningful way to define this elusive quality is to consider the designs of God, for they, along with godly attributes and God himself, are the epitome of excellence.

It was God who raised up the dry land and confined the oceans to their beds. It was he who stirred the seas and made currents, paths, in the watery vastness. It was the great Creator who carefully crafted the veins of every leaf of every tree and bush. He shaped the jewel-like hummingbird and endowed it with the ability to hover and drink the flower's sweet nectar. It was God who fashioned the graceful doe and gifted her with participation in the creation process as she gives birth to her fawns.

Carefully look at the rocks worn smooth by the never-ending river, the stones that are polished to reveal their multitudes of colors and textures. Slowly walk through the field of wildflowers, catch the fragrance, drink in the bouquet of hues. Patiently watch the sun settle down on the layered purple hills, and wonder as the clouds blush at the warmth of the dying rays. Silently move across the pristine whiteness of the first snowfall, and feel the soft crunch of the millions of perfect snowflakes beneath your feet. The designs of God are both endless and excellent.

But the excellence of God's designs is not limited to plants and animals, to seas and sweeping vistas and changing seasons. The ancient singer cried out to God, "When I consider your heavens, the work of your fingers, the moon and the stars, which you have set in place, what is man that you are mindful of him, the son of man that you care for him? You made him a little lower than the heavenly beings and crowned him with glory and honor" (Psalm 8:3-5). The crescendo of God's natural creation is you and me — humanity that somehow was made in his image — until, finally, the eternal God entered our world as a creature, as the one we know as Jesus. We are a maze of marvels, with cardio-vascular, digestive and nervous systems that awe the best of our sciences. The mind, the creative genius of the most ordinary person, makes the most powerful computer pale in comparison.

Neither do God's designs stop with the vast universe that is flung across the light years. Or even the seemingly limitless potential of men and women. It was the eternal God who designed the spiritual life, the church, the family and the governments of people. He created the bond between mother and child. He wrote the hymn that was in a Christian's heart long before it was on paper. He designed and prepared heaven for his elected ones. He devised "faith, hope and love" and everything else we think of as good.

Do we see the designs of God? It does not depend upon our eyes, but upon our heart. We look with our inner beings, not with our optic nerves. And when we look with our spirits, we see infinite layers of wonders. Marvel upon marvel. Love upon love. So we ask, How can we doubt God's love when we see the care with which he prepares every gift? Every cell, every molecule, every atom is a gift. Every galaxy, every star, every planet is a gift. The designs of God are his excellent gifts to each of us.

The Old Testament describes God by saying, "He is the Rock, his works are perfect, and all his ways are just" (Deuteronomy 32:4). And the New Testament assures us, "Every good and perfect gift is from above, coming down from the Father of the heavenly lights, who does not change like shifting shadows" (James 1:17).

"Every good and perfect gift is from above . . . ." That is another way of saying that excellence is from the Father. In fact, all we know — or can know — of excellence comes from attending to God's word and observing his good and perfect gifts.

The longer we live as Christians, the more God seems to reveal to us his intricate and awesome designs. His natural laws are dependable and immutable. Likewise, we understand (sometimes at long last) that God's spiritual laws are also true, universal and absolute. If we break those spiritual laws as individuals or as a nation, we face serious consequences.

Yet, all things — organic, inorganic, social, psychological, spiritual — were created for the children of the Great Father in Heaven. Celebrate his gifts! Give thanks for the excellence of God's marvelous designs.

— Bill Henegar

Reflections

1. "The designs of God are both endless and excellent."

2. "Living Nature, not dull Art
   Shall plan my ways and rule my heart."
   — John Henry Cardinal Newman

3. "The crescendo of God's natural creation is you and me — humanity that somehow was made in his image — until, finally, the eternal God entered our world as a creature, as the one we know as Jesus."

4. "O Lord my God! When I in awesome wonder
    Consider all the works Thy hands have made,
    I see the stars, I hear the mighty thunder,
    Thy pow'r throughout the universe displayed.
    Then sings my soul, my Savior God to Thee;
    How great Thou art, how great Thou art!"
    — Stuart K. Hine

5. "Do we see the designs of God? It does not depend upon our eyes, but upon our heart."

6. "The earth is the Lord's,
    and everything in it,
    the world, and all who live in it;
    for he founded it upon the seas
    and established it upon the waters."— Psalm 24:1, 2

7. "Every good and perfect gift is from above, coming down from the Father of the heavenly lights, who does not change like shifting shadows."— James 1:17

42

Reaching for
Our Personal Best

"Reach for the stars!" People frequently use this expression when they are trying to encourage someone to excel or to be successful. I have long believed that being a child of God demands that we do our very best in everything that we do. There is no place for mediocrity for the Christian. As Christians, we will not offer to the Lord anything less than the best we can offer. In the Old Testament, when the Israelites were asked to offer a sacrifice to the Lord, they were told to give the best they had. There is a song that says, "Give of Your Best to the Master." This is the "rule of thumb" that has always characterized what God wants us to do in all of our response to him — give our very best!

Jesus gave a beautiful lesson in the Parable of the Talents. He spoke of three servants to whom the master entrusted five talents, two talents and one talent, respectively. These talents were given to the servants "each according to his ability" (see Matthew 25:14-30). The servants were expected to invest what they were given and to return it when the master returned. The master, according to the parable, did not expect the servants to do more than they were able to do; this is why he gave to them "each according to his ability." But the master *did* want the servants to perform to their highest ability. This is what the Lord wants us to do.

When the master in the parable mentioned above returned, he called each of the men in for them to return to him the talents each had accumulated. The man with five talents had earned five more; the master gave to him five additional talents as a reward for his diligence. The man with the two talents, likewise, returned the original talents and two additional ones he had earned. The man with the one talent told the master: "I knew that you are a hard man, harvesting where you have not sown and gathering where you have not scattered seed. So I was afraid and went out and hid your talent in the ground. See, here is what belongs to you." But the master told him that "you should have put my money on deposit with the bankers, so that when I returned I would have received it back with interest. Take the talent from him and give it to the one who has ten talents" (Matthew 25:24-28). It is clear from this parable that Jesus is demanding from us our **very best!**

There is no place in God's scheme of things for mediocrity. Someone has said, "Average is not enough; for average is just as close to the bottom as it is to the top." This does not mean that all of us will perform to the same level, because not all of us have the same abilities or talents. The man with the two talents was not expected to earn five; he pleased his master when he earned two. That was the level of his ability. The parable states that each man was given talents "according to his ability."

As a university professor, I demand certain levels of performance from my students. I know when I begin a new class that I do not have a class of students with equal abilities. There are some in the class who are superior students, and if they perform to the level of their ability, they will receive an "A" for their grade. But if a person has an ability less than the "A" or the "B" students, he or she may receive a "C." If that student has performed to the best of his or her ability, the "C" grade is an acceptable grade.

The Christian student, or the Christian employee, is expected by God to do the best that he or she can do. "Give of your best to the Master." This should be our rule of life in everything we do. When we compete in athletics, we should give it our best. When we are hired by an employer to do a task, we should give that employer our best. There is no room for mediocrity for the Christian.

We should constantly "reach for our personal best." And, as we grow throughout life, our abilities will frequently grow with us. When we are ready to complete our lives for God, we should be able to give God our lives and be able to say with the apostle Paul, "I have fought the good fight" (2 Timothy 4:7). Only then can we say that we have reached for our personal best.

— *Morris M. Womack*

Reflections

1. Do you agree with the statement, "Being a child of God demands that we do our very best in everything we do"? If not, why not? If you agree with it, why do you?

2. Why has God always expected the best from his people?

3. "He gives only the worthless gold
   Who gives from a sense of duty."
   — James Russell Lowell

4. Average is not enough; for average is just as close to the bottom as it is the top.

5. Every one of us has been given unique and special gifts and abilities. How will you use yours?

6. Why was the "one-talent man" (see Matthew 25:24-28)
    rebuked by the master in the Parable of the Talents?

7. "Therefore, I urge you, brothers, in view of God's
    mercy, to offer your bodies as living sacrifices, holy
    and pleasing to God — which is your spiritual wor-
    ship."   — Romans 12:1

43

Never Give Up

Sir Winston Churchill was one of the greatest orators of the twentieth century. His home-spun humor, his ability to use the English language and his brusque style made him an unforgettable character. His oratorical excellence has placed his imprint on our times in a way that he will never be forgotten.

While addressing students at Harrow School in October 1941, he said, "**Never give in! Never give in; Never, Never, never, never! In nothing great or small, large or petty give in except to conviction of honor and good sense.**" One can almost hear the deafening silence that followed these words. Those students and faculty listening to him must have sat in awe at his powerful message.

These same words apply to us in our lives: never give in on your professional honesty, on your moral and spiritual integrity, or in your personal convictions regarding God and things eternal and unchangeable. We must never give in or give up. God expects the best of us.

I want to use a slight "take-off" from Churchill's statement and say, "never give up!" It is pretty certain that his statement included the persistence necessary for each individual who expects to be successful in life — **never give up, never give up, never give up!**

In almost every person's life, there are times when we are tempted to just quit. Why endure the suffering? Why continue the struggle? What's it worth anyhow? I am reminded of a wonderful Christian family that has just recently lost the wife and mother of the family to what seems to most of us as a "premature" death. Surely that family will ask many times over the next few weeks, "Why us?" But, that doesn't solve anything.

In the course of my life, I can recall many times when I was ready to just give up. Was it worth all of the many hours spent in study and in gaining an education? Why not just give up? Believe me, I was often tempted to. My life includes many mistakes that I would give worlds to undo (if I had the worlds to give). I was tempted to give up. But friends, family, and most of all my faith in God would not let me. So I plodded on. God will see us through all the trials, if we will only let him.

A life of excellence demands that we find good in all of life. The Corinthian church had much to regret — and much to rejoice over. Paul declared that "you have been enriched in every way" (1 Corinthians 1:7). They were admonished by Paul to rejoice over the things in their lives that were Christlike. But they had much to regret. They lived in the midst of one of the most immoral societies of their day. On a hill within their eyesight was a center of local idolatrous worship, and the temple prostitutes often brought their evil into their midst. Sin was ever-present to them.

After Paul commended them for their good and reproved them for many practices not in keeping with Christian principles, he stated: "Therefore, my dear brothers, stand firm. Let nothing move you. Always give yourselves fully to the work of the Lord because you know that your labor is not in vain" (1 Corinthians 15:58).

Nothing can impede or defeat us if we place our hand in the hand of God. "If God is for us, who can be against us?" (Romans 8:31). There is nothing so certain as success for us when we have God as our partner. The outcome may not always be what we want, but when he is on our side, the outcome will be what is best for us in the long run. Paul tells us that we are victors when God is our partner. "In all these things we are more than conquerors through him who loved us. For I am convinced that neither death nor life, neither angels nor demons, neither the present nor the future, nor any powers, neither height nor depth, nor anything else in all creation, will be able to separate us from the love of God that is in Christ Jesus our Lord" (Romans 8:37-39).

As members of God's family, the church, we can accomplish more than our imagination can conceive. God is not satisfied with mediocrity. He wants us to live victorious lives that glorify him. He has a work for us that we alone can do. Will we ever give up? Ever? Ever?

— *Morris M. Womack*

Reflections

1. "The person who makes a success of living is the one who sees his goal steadily and aims for it unswervingly. That is dedication." — Cecil B. De Mille

2. Consider the race of the tortoise and the hare: the tortoise won the race not because of his speed but because he refused to "give up."

3. "Don't give up. Keep going. There is always a chance that you will stumble into something terrific. I have never heard of anyone stumbling over anything while sitting down." — Ann Landers

4. "You cannot always expect to reach a certain goal, but you can expect to put your greatest effort to reach it." — Anonymous

5. After losing a son in death, I commented that "I don't think I will ever get over this," only to hear my daugh-

ter comment: "I miss him; but I will not let his death ruin my life." How does this comment apply to our dealing with negative things in our lives?

6. "O Jesus, I have promised To serve Thee to the end;
Be Thou forever near me, My Master and my Friend:
I shall not fear the battle If Thou art by my side,
Nor wander from the pathway If Thou wilt be my
guide."   — John E. Bode

7. "Therefore, my dear brothers, stand firm. Let nothing move you. Always give yourselves fully to the work of the Lord, because you know that your labor in the Lord is not in vain."   — 1 Corinthians 15:58

44

Holy Dissatisfaction

*T*his life is about *tension*. For the Christian, it is the tension between living "in the world" and being "of the world." Between being unholy and holier-than-thou. Between the status quo and constant change. Between condemning the person and condoning the sin. On and on the list of extremes could go. But always, the place we find ourselves — or *should* find ourselves — is between the extremes, in *tension*.

I have found that there is a tension, too, in the way we ought to approach excellence in our lives. As we work toward the completion of any task, there are two extreme positions we can occupy: complete satisfaction and utter dissatisfaction. Between them, in tension, is what I would call "holy dissatisfaction."

There are multitudes of people who go about their work with an attitude of satisfaction. Whatever effort they decide to give to the task at hand is considered "good enough." But usually, good enough is not really good enough. None of us would want to roll down the runway with a pilot who decided halfway through the checklist, "Oh, that's good enough."

The "good enough" mentality got the United States into a heap of trouble a couple of decades ago. Our auto workers and executives had drifted into an attitude that tacitly said, "The cars we are producing are good enough for the world." But they were not. And then Japan reminded us of what a car was supposed to be. Fortunately, the American auto industry learned the lesson in time, and today's American cars are some of the best in the world. Ford's motto, "Quality is Job 1" is more than a public relations ploy.

Probably like you, I have seen a lot of this kind of "good-enough" satisfaction in churches. I have seen church events that were so unplanned and so poorly executed that they were embarrassing. And buildings in such need of repair that, if they were houses in our neighborhood, we would complain about how they were depreciating our property. And publications and Bible school materials that would be unacceptable in the world of education or business. And all these slipshod things are done in the name of the God who does all things well, who did not spare the most excellent thing in existence: his own Son.

However, on the other extreme is the "never good enough" mentality. The well-intentioned but always dissatisfied folks who have this attitude never give an inch. They criticize even the best efforts of their brothers and sisters. One wonders how they will ever enjoy heaven!

Parents who have developed this "never good enough" disposition do untold damage to their children. Sometimes they criticize every move their children make. At other times they never say a word — but the children still know it is impossible to satisfy these key people in their lives.

Churches usually have at least a few of these judges in their midst. And they make it tough on the rest. Often the "never-good-enough" people are too busy judging everyone else to pitch in and make things better. They are content to inspect the work of others and point out everyone's inadequacies.

But there is a place of tension between these extremes that can be thought of as "holy dissatisfaction." What is that? It is the attitude that says, "I (we) probably did the best job possible at the moment . . . but I (we) can do better. Because God empowers us to always move upward."

This attitude does not castigate things in the past. But it does say, "We can do better." Those who were old enough at the time will remember the 1960 presidential debate between John F. Kennedy and Richard M. Nixon. Nixon defended the policies of the previous Eisenhower administration — and did an admirable job. However, Kennedy kept hammering away with the words, "I believe we can do better!" It was a brilliant tactic, because his words are always true: We *can indeed* do better.

But "holy dissatisfaction" is more than a debate tactic. It is the commitment to grow in the Lord, to honor him more, to love him more dearly, to serve him more faithfully. It is an attitude that attacks nothing or no one, but simply strives to "press on toward the goal to win the prize for which God has called me heavenward in Christ Jesus" (Philippians 3:14).

If you and I embrace this holy dissatisfaction, it will be all right at times to say, "We have done as much as we can do now — it's *good enough.*" At other times we will want to say, "What we've done is good — but it's *never good enough.*" We will hold a position of tension, which is never an easy place to be.

Our attitude will be expressed: "Even if we give our bodies to be burned, it is not enough. Because God always deserves more. Yet, because of his great love toward us, *we are accepted!*" Our poor deeds and gifts to him are glorious in his sight because they are accompanied by faith and love and a desire to be the best for him. And so, we never rest . . . until we rest in him.

— *Bill Henegar*

Reflections

1. "Living in tension is not easy, but it is often right."

2. "Let us not become weary in doing good, for at the proper time we will reap a harvest if we do not give up."   — Galatians 6:9

3. "If you and I embrace this holy dissatisfaction, it will be all right at times to say, 'We have done as much as we can do now — it's *good enough*.' At other times we will want to say, 'What we've done is good — but it's *never good enough*.'"

4. "Be perfect, therefore, as your heavenly Father is perfect."   — Matthew 5:48

5. "Our poor deeds and gifts to [God] are glorious in his sight because they are accompanied by faith and love and a desire to be the best for him."

6. "What shall we say, then? Shall we go on sinning so that grace may increase? By no means! We died to sin; how can we live in it any longer?" — Romans 6:1, 2

7. "I press on toward the goal to win the prize for which God has called me heavenward in Christ Jesus."
                                    — Philippians 3:14

45

The Magnificent Quest

In my office at Pepperdine University I have a figurine of the Cervantes' character Don Quixote, the man of Castilla de La Mancha. Cervantes, who died as an old soldier and poor gentleman in 1616 within ten days of William Shakespeare's death, portrayed Quixote as a half-crazed man, "scorned and covered with scars," who rode the plains of Castilla La Mancha. With Don Quixote and his faithful squire, Sancho Panza, Cervantes introduced two of the greatest characters in fiction and created one of the most entertaining adventure stories of all time. Don Quixote, who was in his heart a noble and valiant knight, strove valiantly to rid his world of evil, but this man of pure heart could not find evil people to fight so he jousted with windmills. However, the book is much more than a joust with windmills. Through his wonderful story, Cervantes is able to teach us about the power of life lived out as a magnificent quest in pursuit of God's excellence.

The story begins with Quixote's seeking to find his lady, for a knight without a lady is like a tree without leaves or a body without a soul or a life without a purpose. At a village near his own he met a farm girl named Aldonza Lorenzo. To us her name itself seems to convey the soiled, ugly nature of her life. This young woman was a tramp at best, prostitute at worst. The light of hope had long since died in her eyes. Like so many others who have been defeated by life's struggles, she just survived any way she could.

Actually, I tend to confuse the Cervantes' book with the famous play by Dale Wassermann, *The Man of La Mancha*. The play is based roughly on the book and its message of courage and hope. In Wassermann's play about Don Quixote, one song sung by the hero and some time later by Aldonza is "Dulcinea," the bright and shining one. It is with this naive purity that the lonely knight sings to his lady and dreams of her beauty gracing his castle. She protests. She calls him crazy, but the play ends with her claim to the name and the dream. She is reborn. She is forever the lady, bright and shining.

What is it that beats us down, convinces us that we are "Aldonzas," fools, failed or flawed? Does our defeat stem from words laughingly, though thoughtlessly, spoken by a relative or friend, "You're about the dumbest person I know." Does defeat derive from our own futile comparisons of ourselves to those perceived as most beautiful or successful? Is it just our remembrance of past failures at sports, academics or love? Is it just life itself? Whatever it is, many seem to end up without hope, devastated by life.

The critical issue is, what can make life an exciting adventure or a meaningful quest? What is it that can create in us a Quixote-type heart that is pure, brave and bold? I believe that the answer lies in the power of dreams. The famous poet Langston Hughes wrote, "Hold fast to dreams, my friends, for if dreams die, life is a broken-winged bird that cannot fly." Life without a passionate quest, a dream-capturing heart and soul, is broken. Life lived with vision and hope is a bold adventure.

The old man of La Mancha had a dream. It captured his heart and caused an insignificant old man to traipse around the countryside touching others and lifting the fallen, mending the broken. In Wassermann's play, Quixote sings another song, one capturing the heart of dreams. Through the words of the song, we are encouraged to see that our dreams are only worthwhile when they cause us to reach beyond ourselves, to the seemingly unobtainable. I teach and preach in the hopes that my students and my listeners will learn to sing the poet's song:

This is my quest — to follow that star,
No matter how hopeless, no matter how far. . . .
To be willing to march into hell for a heavenly cause!
And the world will be better for this —
That one man scorned and covered with scars
Still strove with his last ounce of courage
To reach the unreachable stars!

If you do not possess in your heart of hearts a dream which drives and motivates your life, begin right now to formulate one. Flaws and failures are but building blocks to successful living for men and women motivated to love and laugh and lift others, and to dream of brighter tomorrows. Bright tomorrows are always built on failed yesterdays. As you develop your dream, make it an impossible dream. Make it one that stretches you and drives you to new heights. Make it one that you can only achieve if God blesses it. Make it one that is noble, pure, true and just. If you do, your life will be filled with music and grace, and you can turn Aldonzas into Dulcineas, bright and beautiful.

— L. Keith Whitney

Reflections

1. "Hold fast to dreams, my friends, for if dreams die, life is a broken-winged bird that cannot fly."
   — Langston Hughes

2. Bright tomorrows are built on failed yesterdays.

3. If a knight without a lady is like a tree without leaves or a body without a soul or a life without a purpose, then much more a man or woman without a dream.

4. "Where there is no vision, the people perish."
                                                   — Proverbs 29:18

5. "The man who radiates good cheer, who makes life happier wherever he meets it, is always a man of vision and faith."   — Ella Wheeler Wilcox

6. "A task without a vision is drudgery. A vision without a task is a dream. A task with a vision is victory."
                                                   — A saying

7. "But you will receive power when the Holy Spirit comes on you; and you will be my witnesses in Jerusalem, and in all Judea and Samaria, and to the ends of the earth."   — Acts 1:8

Things That Are PRAISEWORTHY

46

Rim of the World

*H*igh in the San Bernardino Mountains east of Los Angeles is a two-lane road called "Rim of the World Highway." At one point, the road winds along the crest of the mountains, with the terrain radically falling off on both sides. It can give you a slightly uncomfortable feeling. As your car serpentines along, there is no embankment on your right or left as usual in mountain driving. Neither are there fields or hills spreading out to your right or left as on the plain. Instead, your car almost feels like an airplane, slipping along with lofty views of valleys and deserts far below.

Like the tightrope walker, the Rim of the World Highway traverses a narrow and hazardous path. There is no room for substantial error. If you pay more attention to the vistas than to the band of asphalt before you, you may end up a few thousand feet down the mountain.

The Rim of the World Highway is not so very different from the Christian life in some respects. In Christ, we are called to walk a balanced life that twists and turns between some very tempting vistas. Over and over, we find the truth of Jesus in the center, between two extremes that beckon to us with rational or emotional appeals.

It is interesting that Jesus was viewed in many different ways by people with widely differing perspectives on life. A Roman centurion viewed him as the Lord who had been given remarkable authority, who was too holy to come under the centurion's roof. Demon-possessed men who lived among the tombs viewed Jesus as the Son of God, who was coming to torture them. Some teachers of the law were convinced that Jesus was a blasphemer of God. A woman with a twelve-year hemorrhage believed that he was a healer and that even touching the edge of his cloak might cure her. The Pharisees thought of Jesus as a lawbreaker who violated the Mosaic codes. Some of them even thought he was in league with Satan, who gave him the power to drive out demons. The "religious" viewed Jesus as nothing more than a glutton and drunkard, a friend of the hated tax collectors and other sinners. Ordinary folk recognized him as a prophet. A few knew him as the savior of the world.

Based on these and other descriptions, how would a personality expert today profile Jesus? Certainly, the expert would conclude that Jesus had stood society on its ear. Many people of Jesus' day simply did not know what to do with him. He seemed to turn his world upside down. In reality, the world was already upside down, and Jesus was righting the world. He was, indeed, the most balanced person who ever lived. But when everyone else is falling, the one standing firm appears to be falling instead.

Jesus often gave his hearers the conventional wisdom of the day, followed by God's widsom. For example, he said, "You have heard it was said to the people long ago, 'Do not murder, and anyone who murders will be subject to judgment.'" Then he added, "But *I tell you* that anyone who is angry with his brother will be subject to judgment." Again, Jesus knew the way people thought; he said, "You have heard that it was said, 'Love your neighbor and hate your enemy.'" Thus it has always been: Patriotism . . . nationalism . . . tribalism. . . . Love your own people. . . . Band together to oppose all outsiders. "But *I tell you*," said Jesus, "Love your enemies and pray for those who persecute you, that you may be sons of your Father in heaven."

Jesus is a picture of apparent contrasts: strong yet gentle, holy yet familiar, separate from the world yet deeply involved in it. He loved weddings and family affairs, yet he was a "man of sorrows and acquainted with grief." The New Testament paints a portrait of him that suggests he lived life to the fullest, with joy in every step. And yet, he did not turn away from a course that would result in an "early" death as a young man not much beyond 30 years of age. His life was short. But full of eternity.

You and I must remember that we are not merely spectators, observers of Jesus. We are participants. We live *in him*. We walk as he walked.

In Ephesians 5:15, 16, Paul wrote, "Be very careful, then, how you live — not as unwise but as wise, making the most of every opportunity, because the days are evil." The old King James Bible is a little closer to a literal translation of the passage; it says, "See then that ye walk circumspectly, not as fools, but as wise . . . ." Paul literally said, *"Look carefully"* or *circumspectly* — that is, look all around.

Those who are wise *look all around* themselves, spiritually, as they walk through life. *They live a life of careful balance* — like Jesus. Because they are walking the rim of the world.

— *Bill Henegar*

Reflections

1. "Over and over we find the truth of Jesus in the center, between two extremes that beckon to us with rational and emotional appeals."

2. "For John came neither eating nor drinking, and they say, 'He has a demon.' The Son of Man came eating

and drinking, and they say, 'Here is a glutton and a drunkard, a friend of tax collectors and "sinners."' But wisdom is proved right by her actions."

— Matthew 11:18, 19

3. "You and I must remember that we are not merely spectators, observers of Jesus. We are participants. We live *in him*. We walk as he walked."

4. "Wisdom is greater than knowledge,
    for wisdom includes knowledge and the due use of
    it."   — Joseph Burritt Sevelli Capponi

5. "Be very careful, then, how you live — not as unwise but as wise, making the most of every opportunity, because the days are evil."   — Ephesians 5:15, 16

6. "Those who are wise *look all around* themselves, spiritually, as they walk through life."

7. "Do not deceive yourselves. If anyone of you thinks he is wise by the standards of this age, he should become a 'fool' so that he may become wise. For the wisdom of this world is foolishness in God's sight."

— 1 Corinthians 3:18, 19

47

Well Done, Faithful Servant

All of us like to be appreciated. One of three interpersonal needs that all humans tend to have is the need to be accepted, the need to be needed. The coach often slaps a player on his backside as he leaves the ball game, especially if the player has played well. We hear a good speaker, and we want to compliment her. We show our children our appreciation in many ways for the things they do to make us proud of them. It is a common thing for us to show such appreciation.

In the Parable of the Ten Minas (or Pounds), when the first servant returned after having made his investment grow considerably, he was told by the master, "'Well done, my good servant,' his master replied, 'Because you have been trustworthy in a very small matter, take charge of ten cities'" (Luke 19:17). The same message comes through in the Parable of the Talents. Recall that, before going on a journey, the master gave to three of his servants five, two and one talents, respectively. Jesus said in the Parable: "After a long time the master of those servants returned and settled accounts with them. The man who had received the five talents brought the other five. 'Master,' he said, 'you entrusted me with five talents. See, I have gained five more.' The master told him, 'Well done, good and faithful servant! You have been faithful with a few things; I will put you in charge of many things'" (Matthew 25:19-21). He made the same statement to the two-talent man who had doubled his investment.

All of us need recognition, but not all of us behave in a manner that will cause our master to say such laudatory words to us. Our Master, Jesus Christ, wants to have the same things to say to us, but he expects us to perform in a manner that will make him proud of us. We need to do works of obedience that will demonstrate the strength of our faith. Then, he will recognize us and give us the reward he has promised.

There are several lessons that we can learn from the above statements from the parables, and from the fact that Jesus wants us to obey him. First, in the story recorded by Matthew after the Parable of the Talents is Jesus' warning **there will be a day of reckoning** about the final judgment. We shall all stand in the presence of God to answer for our deeds in the flesh. It will be a fearsome and awful day for those who are unprepared to meet the Master. Second, **God expects us to be productive.** We must do our best to make God proud of us. Only then will he "pat us on the back" and tell us that we have done well. Third, **those who do not perform to God's approval will be punished.** Just as the one-talent man was cast into outer darkness because he was not productive and did not perform well, so also we will be rejected if we do not obey our Master. God does not expect perfection from us, but he does expect obedience and effort.

The final days of the life of the apostle Paul are certainly an example for us. When he wrote his second letter to Timothy, he recognized that his days on earth were coming to an end. He wrote these words: "For I am already being poured out like a drink offering, and the time has come for my departure. I have fought the good fight, I have finished the race, I have kept the faith. Now there is in store for me the crown of righteousness, which the Lord, the righteous Judge, will award to me on that day — and not only to me, but also to all who have longed for his appearing" (2 Timothy 4:6-8). What a way to face death: with hope and assurance for approval by our Judge! We should all long to be faithful in order to hear the words of Jesus, "Come you who are blessed by my Father; take your inheritance, the kingdom prepared for you since the creation of the world" (Matthew 25:34). As an old song says, "What a day of rejoicing that will be."

I admonish you as you read these words: Give diligence to finish this life with the approval of the God of all creation. All the riches of the world and all the power that Satan can give us is not to be compared with the reward that God has prepared for us. Hold out your hands and offer your heart to him; he will never let you down.

— *Morris M. Womack*

Reflections

1. Being a faithful servant means more than having faith that God exists; it involves being responsive to what he expects us to do or to be.

2. "Be faithful, even to the point of death, and I will give you the crown of life." — Revelation 2:10

3. "He that is faithful in that which is least is faithful also in much; and he that is unjust in the least is unjust also in much." — Luke 16:10

4. "Let us have faith that right makes might; and in that faith, let us, to the end, dare to do our duty as we understand it." — Abraham Lincoln

5. The faith that stands in the Final Judgment is that which exercises itself in the small and mundane things of daily living; "it is required that those who have been given a trust must prove faithful."

6. "We may suffer loss of wealth, but we are rich in Christ. We may suffer death. But we will receive a crown of life."   — Lawrence O. Richards

7. "Now fear the Lord and serve him with all faithfulness. Throw away the gods your forefathers worshiped beyond the River and in Egypt, and serve the LORD" (Joshua 24:14). Do we **today** have "gods" that we need to throw away?

48

A Way Worth Traveling

*T*he young man stood in my doorway at Pepperdine University and asked if he might have a few minutes of my time. He said he was gathering information for a speech in a college class on public speaking. The assignment was to present an oral biography of a great person, and he had chosen to speak on Howard A. White, fifth president of Pepperdine. He had been referred to me by his advisor who knew that Dr. White had been not only my friend and mentor, but my hero as well.

"Sure, I'll be glad to tell you what I can about Dr. White," I said. We sat down in my office, and I began sharing with him some general information on our late president: his academic background, his predecessor and successor, his accomplishments and so on. As I spoke of the great professor and university administrator, I was reminded of the reasons for my admiration and love for him. Memories of him warmed me — images of him sprang to life and were caught by the senses of my mind. Once again I could hear his strong, resonant voice with its rich and articulate intonations. I could feel his firm handshake, his welcoming disposition. I could see his mannerisms: the slight limp that betrayed the pain in his hip, the crooked smile, the ready laugh that shook his entire frame — and his closed eyes and tilted-back head as he enjoyed the laugh to the fullest.

After several minutes of reflection, I moved beyond the surface aspects of Dr. White's life, and I began to search for ways to describe his character. First, I confessed to the student that this man, though not necessarily impressive physically, was one of my greatest heroes. I thought out loud about the essence of his life. Then I summarized: "I guess I would say that Dr. White was a man of noble character. A true Christian gentleman."

I tried to think of other ways to paint a portrait of his spirit, but I really didn't succeed. It was the best description I could give. Still, it somehow sounded inadequate in the midst of this verbose, multiple-adjectived culture of ours — a culture that overflows with words like "awesome, fantastic, incredible, extraordinary and phenomenal."

But how better could I say it? He was indeed a noble, Christian gentleman. And that is no small thing. To be **noble** means to demonstrate high moral ideals, to possess excellent or superior qualities. It means greatness of character. To be a **gentleman** means to be a courteous, gracious man with a strong sense of honor. And finally, to be a **Christian** means to confess Jesus Christ as Lord and Savior and to live a life worthy of the call of Christ. It seemed to me that those words describe Howard White very well. Even if they are rarely used today.

To be noble, to be a gentleman or gentlewoman, to be a Christian. When you think about it, can there be a better epitaph than those words? I can find none — not even "President of the United States."

But how do you and I, how do ordinary people earn such an admirable epitaph? I believe that kind of reputation is earned one day at a time, one decision at a time, one gracious act at a time. And after a lifetime of small kindnesses, gracious acts and honest words, perhaps someone will finally add those things up and conclude that we, too, were noble and faithful.

Is it worth the effort? Oh, yes! It is a goal worthy of our unfailing efforts. As Don Quixote sang in *Man of La*

Mancha, ". . . and the world will be better for this, that one man, scorned and covered with scars, still strove with his last ounce of courage to reach the unreachable stars."

To live nobly and faithfully is to live with this thought before us every day: "I must seek and then take the high road, the moral and gracious way, the narrow path of faith in the One who makes us righteous by his own unique righteousness."

For me, it helps to think of heroes like Howard Ashley White, who took the high road much more often than he chose the low one. I thank that young man who prompted me to think again about my mentor and friend. And I like to think that my reminiscences might just encourage the young man to join me in a daily walk — and struggle — to live a noble, gentle and faithful life.

— *Bill Henegar*

Reflections

1. "Nobility is the one and only virtue."
   — Decimus Junius Juvenalis (Juvenal)

2. "And after a lifetime of small kindnesses, gracious acts and honest words, perhaps someone will finally add those things up and conclude that we, too, were noble and faithful."

3. "His life was gentle, and the elements
   So mixed in him that Nature might stand up
   And say to all the world, 'This was a man!'"
   — William Shakespeare

4. "To live nobly and faithfully is to live with this thought before us every day: 'I must seek and then take the high road, the moral and gracious way, the

narrow path of faith in the One who makes us righteous by his own unique righteousness.'"

5. "Noble be man
    Helpful and good!
    For that alone
    Sets him apart
    From every other creature
    On earth."   — Johann Wolfgang von Goethe

6. "And the world will be better for this, that one man,
    scorned and covered with scars, still strove with his
    last ounce of courage to reach the unreachable stars."
                                                     — Joe Darion

7. "Be good, sweet maid, and let who will be clever;
    Do noble things, not dream them, all day long;
    And so make Life, and Death, and that For Ever
    One grand sweet song."   — Charles Kingsley

49

Respect for Others

I have previously expressed my gratitude to Pepperdine University, my employer, for the opportunity to teach in its Heidelberg, Germany, program. Our facility in Heidelberg is housed in a mansion built at the turn of the century for a wealthy industrialist. It is located in a heavily wooded area near the famous castle ruins on a hill overlooking the old city. The castle grounds include gardens and walking paths. One area includes a plaque in memory of Johann Wolfgang von Goethe, who strolled the gardens years before. I often spent time reading his works as I walked along the same dusty paths and watched the barges on the Neckar River below.

Goethe wrote, "Human relations means treating people as if they were what they ought to be, for thereby you help them to become what they are capable of being." Isn't that what respect is all about? Respect, I believe, involves showing more concern for people than agendas, thinking highly of others, building them up in love and treating everyone with fairness and integrity. Romans 12:10 puts it this way: "Love each other with genuine affection, and take delight in honoring each other."

Respecting other persons means that we are willing to listen to the input and thoughts of those who are different from us. It means that we resist an attitude of superiority. Respect stems from true humility, ". . . thinking of others as better than yourself" (Philippians 2:3 NLT). Respect recognizes someone else's worth as God's unique creation; it honors the other person for who he or she is. It is true humility because respect requires us to make the other person look good without trying to elevate ourselves at the same time. Respect grows in us as we recognize two things: (1) Beneath the veneer, we are all quite similar, and (2) God created us to serve, not to rule over others. True leaders, the ones everyone respects, serve.

An old woman — insignificant, her name long ago forgotten, and a lonely resident of a geriatric ward in an English hospital — penned words that help us to understand the first of the underpinnings of respect. She addressed the following poem to the people who surrounded her in her last days.

What do you see? What do you see?
Are thinking when you look at me —
A crabbed old woman, not very wise,
Uncertain of habit with far away eyes,
· · ·
Who resisting or not lets you do as you will
With bathing and feeding, the long day to fill.
Is that what you're thinking, is that what you see?
Then open your eyes, you're not looking at me.
[She recites her memories of life, then . . .]
The body it crumbles, grace and vigor depart.
There is a stone where I once had a heart.
But inside this old carcass a young girl still dwells,
And now again my bittered heart swells.
I remember the joys, I remember the pain
And I'm loving and living life over again,
· · ·
So open your eyes, open and see
Not a crabbed old woman,
Look closer — see *me*!

Inside each of us is forever the child. We long to be significant, somebody valued, a person of worth. Respect demands that we look at the other and try to really see who he or she is on the inside. It demands that we care enough to want to know what the other thinks, what he or she feels.

But true respect grows only from a servant's heart and a giving spirit. Colonel James B. Irwin, former astronaut and part of the crew that made a successful moon walk, helped me understand that heart. Addressing the National Religious Broadcasters Convention in Washington, D.C., he spoke of the thrill of his adventure, of watching earthrise one day and of his realization that many would consider him a celebrity upon his return. Humbled by the awesome goodness of Almighty God, Colonel Irwin shared his feelings with the audience: "As I was returning to earth, I realized that I was a servant, not a celebrity. So I am here as God's servant on planet Earth to share what I have experienced that others might know the glory of God."

Respect for others really comes when we break loose from the limits of our earth-ties and see the magnificence of God and his love for us. As we see Jesus, the Divine Servant who girded himself with a towel and washed his disciples' feet, we clearly understand the importance of others and the necessity of serving. Any one of the disciples would gladly have washed the feet of the Master, their Lord and Messiah, but to take up the towel meant they would have to serve one another. The One who humbled himself and became obedient to death itself took up the towel and served. Will we ever learn the lesson? We are not born to stardom; we are reborn to serve!

— *L. Keith Whitney*

Reflections

1. "Human relations means treating people as if they were what they ought to be, for thereby you help them to become what they are capable of being."
   — Goethe

2. "Love each other with genuine affection, and take delight in honoring each other."   — Romans 12:10

3. Respect stems from true humility, ". . . thinking of others as better than yourself" (Philippians 2:3 NLT).

4. Respect recognizes someone else's worth as God's unique creation; it honors the other person for who he or she is.

5. True respect grows only from a servant's heart and a giving spirit.

6. Respect grows in us as we recognize two things:
   (1) Beneath the veneer we are quite similar, and
   (2) God created us to serve not to rule over others.

7. "Do you understand what I am doing? You call me 'Teacher' and 'Lord,' and you are right, because it is true. And since I, the Lord and Teacher, have washed your feet, you ought to wash each other's feet."
   — John 14:12b-14, NLT

50

Godliness with Contentment

$\mathcal{O}$ne of the great maladies of our day is the amount of discontent that we experience in our lives. In almost any bookstore, you find books on contentment, on how to live at peace with yourself and similar subjects comprising a comparatively large section. The apostle Paul must have realized that this is one of the weaknesses of the flesh. He admonished the young preacher Timothy: "Godliness with contentment is great gain. For we brought nothing into the world, and we can take nothing out of it. But if we have food and clothing, we will be content with that" (1 Timothy 5:6-8). The disposition that Paul is admonishing us to have is very rare in this world. We never seem to have enough; we have not learned the great art of contentment.

Developing contentment *is* an art. Paul said so himself. He had many reasons to be discontent, from a human point of view. He had forsaken family, fame and fortune in order to serve God. He is thought by many to have been trained to be a great rabbi in the Jewish faith. He describes his lofty position in life in Philippians 3:1-6. You may want to read that reference. After describing his status, he stated that "whatever was to my profit I now consider loss for the sake of Christ" (Philippians 3:7). Later on, Paul describes how he developed his Christian attitude. He wrote: ". . . I have learned to be content whatever the circumstances. I know what it is to be in need, and I know what it is to have plenty. I have learned the secret of being content in any and every situation, whether well fed or hungry, whether living in plenty or in want. I can do everything through him who gives me strength" (Philippians 4:11-13).

We need to stress three things from Paul's situation. First, he had experienced both good and bad; both a life of plenty and of need. Second, he **learned the secret** of how to be content. It is not a gift that God gives us or something we can buy. It is something we must learn. Third, he discovered that he could do all things with the help of Jesus Christ. Not until we have recognized our position in life, realized that we need to do something about it and placed our lives under the control of him who died for our sins, can we really win the victory.

There is a distinct difference between "satisfaction" and "contentment." Our appetites — physical, social and spiritual — are almost insatiable. When we seem to satisfy a desire, good though it may be, there seems to be a greater appetite for greater satisfaction. For example, if we have the goal of earning a certain amount of money, when we reach that goal, then we want to earn even more. So, it seems, we are never able to totally satisfy our desires. Contentment, on the other hand, is a frame of mind that we acquire or, to use Paul's statement, "learn." We can learn to be contented.

It is extremely important that we "learn the secret" of being content. We are never able to totally control our environment or the events of our lives. It is true that we have a certain amount of control over what happens to us. But, we can never **totally** control the events that shape our lives. This is why Paul tells the young preacher Timothy that "godliness with contentment is great gain."

It is vital that we place our lives under the control of our Master, Jesus Christ. Let him help us to "learn the secret" of being content. This world with all of its allurements can never satisfy or make us totally content. "Things" can never bring contentment. Some of the wealthiest people in the world are some of the most miserable. "Knowledge" cannot bring contentment. There must be a training of the mind. We must have our desires and aspirations under control. We must be able to train our minds to be content with what we have. I used to hear that there are only two types of things that we should or could worry about: things we can help and things that we cannot help. The things we cannot help, we can do nothing about them; we simply must learn to live with them. The things we *can* help, we should get ourselves involved in changing or helping them.

A person who has his or her life under control is one who has learned to live with what he or she has. I have seen people in many countries living on many different levels of existence. We must learn that in whatever "state of life" that we find ourselves, we should be content. My prayer for all of us is that we let Christ control our lives. He will help us attain the state of contentment if we will practice godliness.

— *Morris M. Womack*

Reflections

1. In what way(s) can contentment be regarded as an art? Can I learn this art if I put my heart to it?

2. "In this world there are only two tragedies. One is not getting what one wants, and the other is getting it."
— Oscar Wilde

3. "For we brought nothing into the world, and we can take nothing out of it. But if we have food and clothing, we will be content with that" (1 Timothy 5:6-7). Study this along with Job 1:21.

4. We are never able to totally control our environment, nor the events of our lives, nor to provide total satisfaction; however, we do have the ability with Christ's help to develop contentment.

5. "But seek first his kingdom and his righteousness, and all these things will be given to you as well. Therefore do not worry about tomorrow, for tomorrow will worry about itself. Each day has enough trouble of its own."   — Matthew 6:33, 34

6. A person who has his or her life under control is one who has learned to live with what he/she has.

51

Noblesse Oblige: To Live with Honor

*H*onor is a high-sounding word, isn't it? When I hear someone speak about honor, I think about those who died as prisoners of war without revealing national secrets or betraying their fellow soldiers. Honor is living faithfully under a sense of obligation or duty. But what factors lead to an attitude of honor; what do we need to realize?

*H*aving chosen to end life centered on me, revolving around my *needs,* my wants and my abilities, I have been crucified with Christ Jesus my Lord. Indeed, the life I now live in the body I live by faith in my Lord who loved me and sacrificed himself for me. (See Galatians 2:20.) Having then the Spirit of Sonship alive inside my body, I choose to live to the praise of his glorious grace. I live to bring honor to the Father.

*O*nly those who are fully aware that God has adopted them into his family, only those in whom God's Spirit testifies with their spirits that they are God's children, princes and princesses in his household, fully accept the obligation of royalty. Only when we recognize that we are born again into the most glorious family of all — God's family — will we accept the responsibility to live to bring glory to his name.

Noblesse Oblige is what the French aristocracy called it. Those of noble birth, those born with great privilege, had an obligation to live nobly. But all you have to do to understand our status as royal heirs is to read the eighth chapter of the book of Romans. We are adopted into the family of God; we are joint heirs with Jesus.

*O*bligation is a compelling word. *Noblesse oblige* is forever and always obligation. It is the obligation of honorable, generous and responsible behavior. It is the behavior of belief. It is the behavior of faith in God the Father. It is the only logical way of life for one born again to such noble position as Sonship.

*R*oyalty born of God must honor the behavior of Jesus. Sons and daughters of the Father of All Mercies must adhere to the highest standards of justice and love. But all that sounds very *theological,* doesn't it? It sounds high and mighty, but it kind of begs the question, doesn't it? After all, *our real problem is determining what it means to live with honor.* Practically speaking, what does it mean to live to the praise of his glorious grace?

In ancient times when life's pace was much slower, monks withdrew into an antiseptic circle and, within sterile walls, found little else to do but make lists of sins. They categorized sins. Seven they classified as most deadly of all. One of these so-called deadly sins, one so bad it could reach out from hell itself and capture the soul for Satan, was called *sloth.* Although popular meaning seems to suggest laziness, sloth is much more akin to apathy. It is to see suffering or injustice and do nothing. Further, it is to do nothing because we simply don't care.

The attitude accompanying sloth led German Christians to be content with piety and religion while Hitler practiced genocide. Rolf Hockhuth's controversial play *The Deputy* gets to the heart of our obligation to God and others. In the play a young priest named Ricardo is fed up with the apathy of the Church and Christians generally. As he pins the Star of David on his vestments and joins a carload of Jews being taken to the gas chamber, he explains:

> To look on idly when tomorrow morning our fellow citizens . . . are loaded aboard cattle cars.

Are we to stand by and wave our handkerchiefs to
them?
And then — then we go home?
Confess — what should we confess?
That we have used the name of God in vain! . . .
And then on Sunday morning we ring the bells
and celebrate our Mass so filled with sacred
thoughts, that nothing . . . tempts us to consider
those . . . being driven into the gas.

We dare not draw an antiseptic circle around life and
call it "church" or "religion." As his children, we are to
live with honor. We are to act justly and to love mercy.
We are to care. We are under obligation as children of
God, joint heirs with Jesus the First Born, to live to the
praise of the Father's glorious grace. We are to live to
bring honor to the Father.

— *L. Keith Whitney*

Reflections

1. "The burning conviction that we have a holy duty
   toward others is often a way of attaching our drowning selves to a passing raft."   — Eric Hoffer

2. "Familiar acts are beautiful through love."
                                 — Percy Bysshe Shelley

3. "Lord, grant that I might not so much seek to be loved
   as to love."   — Saint Francis of Assisi

4. "Existence is a strange bargain. Life owes us little; we
   owe it everything. The only true happiness comes
   from squandering ourselves for a purpose."
                                 — William Cowper

5. "Having then the Spirit of Sonship alive inside my body, I choose to live to the praise of his glorious grace. I will live to bring honor to the Father."

6. "*Noblesse Oblige* is forever and always obligation. It is the obligation of honorable, generous and responsible behavior."

7. "Sons and daughters of the Father of All Mercies must adhere to the highest standards of justice and love."

52

Peace Like a River

*W*hen I was a teenager, my dad conducted "Singing Schools" for surrounding churches. He often said that one of his favorite songs was "When Peace Like a River." Last night I dreamed of my Dad, and when I chose this title to write about, I thought of his favorite hymn. As I contemplated this, I called and asked my son what his favorite song is and he replied, "When Peace Like A River." There are several songs that we sing that battle for first place with me, but I must say that this one is extremely near the top.

The chorus to this song is especially comforting: "It is well . . . with my soul." When you really think about it, what is more to be desired than for it "to be well with my soul"? We can amass many great treasures for ourselves: wealth, fame, friendships, power, influence — to name only a few of the things for which men strive. All of these are empty and fruitless if we cannot control our own minds. I think so often of Solomon. He had all of the above blessings. God gave them to him for asking for wisdom with which to govern his people (see 1 Kings 1:4-15). But Solomon was far from having inner peace, or "peace like a river."

Life was a little simpler for me when we lived in the suburbs of Detroit, Michigan. A friend would often call me to say, "Let's go fishing." We would go to one of the nearby rivers that meandered through the meadows of southwestern Wayne County. And we fished. We didn't catch much, but that didn't matter. We would throw our baited hooks in the water, lie back on the sloping bank of the river and wait. Often, we didn't even talk much. We would listen to the babbling of the brook (or river) and at times go to sleep. Now, that is "peace like a river."

The Bible speaks of "peace like a river." In his book, *The Major Prophets*, James E. Smith writes this explanation of the closing chapters of Isaiah: "After describing the present gloom, Isaiah soars again in to the heights of prophetic expectancy regarding the glorious plans which God had for his people on the other side of captivity." It is within this context that Isaiah wrote, "For this is what the Lord says: 'I will extend peace to her like a river, and the wealth of nations like a flooding stream; you will nurse and be carried on her arm and dangled on her knees. As a mother comforts her child, so will I comfort you; and you will be comforted over Jerusalem. When you see this, your heart will rejoice and you will flourish like grass; the hand of the Lord will be known to his servants, but his fury will be shown to his foes" (Isaiah 66:12-14).

There truly is something very calming about sitting down beside a stream of water. Scripture uses this analogy often. The "city" of our eternal existence with God has a river. When John was describing his revelation of heaven, he wrote, "Then the angel showed me the river of the water of life, as clear as crystal, flowing from the throne of God and of the Lamb down the middle of the great street of that city" (Revelation 22:1-2a).

I have not always been able to fully appreciate the beauty of the idea of "It is Well," though I have always wanted to. Many times, I ask students, "If you could have anything in the world, what would you choose?" Of course I have heard all of the expected answers: money, great job, success, great future, power and so on. But I then ask, "Would all of this make you happy?" In more pensive moments, many of these same students say, "I would rather have happiness, contentment." Isn't this what it's all about?

Paul had reason to become bitter at the world. He gave up fame, fortune and power to become a slave of God. He could have become very bitter: I gave up all I had for **this**? But in that great love letter to the Philippian Church, he cried out, "**I have learned the secret** of being content in any and every situation. . . . I can do everything through him who gives me strength" (Philippians 4:12-13).

You too can become at peace with yourself and with God. Letting God possess you and control you and comfort you is possible. Learn from Paul; learn from great people of God. Someday when I sit down by the river of life with God's people, then I want to drink deeply from the springs of spiritual strength that God provides. Then I want to cry out with great exultation "*It is well with my soul,*" until eternity ceases to exist.

— *Morris M. Womack*

Reflections

1. "Great peace have they who love your law, and nothing can make them stumble." — Psalm 119:165

2. "Now may the Lord of peace himself give you peace at all times and in every way." — 2 Thessalonians 3:16

3. "If you want inner peace find it in solitude, not speed, and if you would find yourself, look to the land from which you came and to which you go."
   — Steward L. Udall

4. "The peace of God which transcends all understanding, will guard your hearts and your minds in Christ Jesus."   — Philippians 4:7

5. "Peace, Perfect peace, in this dark world of sin:
   The blood of Jesus whispers peace within."
                                           — Edward H. Bickersteth

6. "There is a place of quiet rest,
   Near to the heart of God,
   A place where sin cannot molest,
   Near to the heart of God.
   There is a place of comfort sweet,
   Near to the heart of God,
   A place where we our Savior meet,
   Near to the heart of God."   — Cleland B. McAfee

7. "They will beat their swords into plowshares, and their spears into pruning hooks. Nation will not lift up sword against nation, nor will they train for war anymore."   — Isaiah 2:4